ARGO

A. R. WILLIAMS

ISBN 978-1-0980-7804-1 (paperback)
ISBN 978-1-0980-7805-8 (digital)

Christian Faith Publishing, Inc.
832 Park Avenue
Meadville, PA 16335
www.christianfaithpublishing.com

Printed in the United States of America

AUTHOR'S NOTE

This is a story of overcoming evil. So often we let the tests and trials and mishaps of life take us out of character to the point of us doing the unthinkable. And sometimes we let our situations, past or present, determine who we are. Jesus gave his life so we didn't have to stay broken and defeated, bound by evil. If we just give our lives over to the Lord, he can turn any situation around. For with God, anything is possible.

PROLOGUE

"Good morning, Ora."

My eyes fluttered open to see my favorite guard. I smiled at Alonso and closed my eyes once more.

"Good morning, Lonso."

"Oh no, you need to get up, little lady, before your breakfast gets cold."

I began to fake snore until I heard his footsteps fading away. "No, wait!" I yelled as I jumped up and skipped to my cell door. He turned around smiling and handed me my breakfast through the opening. *Scrambled eggs and strawberry pancakes, yummy.* I carefully carried it to my table and walked back to get my water.

"I have a special surprise for you, little one."

My eyes darted up, and I squealed with glee. I set my water on the ground and cupped both my hands through the opening. He placed a small pouch with holes in my hands. I unzipped the pouch and reached inside. An adorable white rat squeaked as he sniffed my hand.

"Oh thank you, Lonso! I love him!"

He smiled and mussed my wild hair. "Happy fifth birthday, Ora."

I woke up screaming like I do every morning. Night after night, I have the same dream where I'm being chased and being dragged out of my mother's arms. It always ends the same with a man in black clothing carrying me away while another drags my mother in the opposite direction. She had dark-brown skin and bright purple eyes that never stopped staring at me. I sat up and rubbed the gook from my eyes that were so much like my mother's. I walked over to the sink and splashed cold water onto my brown face trying to subdue the memories. I stared at my reflection in the mirror as I watched the water drip off my face and onto the counter. *I have to remember to ask Lonso to retwist my locks,* I thought as I touched my hair. He'd started them for me after he saw how unruly my hair was getting in this place. I took a few locks and twisted them together around my head and began to brush my teeth when I heard the sound of a large heavy door creak open and shut with a loud thud.

"Why, hello there, beautiful." I rolled my eyes and didn't bother looking up. "That's no way to speak to the man who brings you breakfast in bed." I snorted and spit in the sink. I walked to the bar and reached for my plate. "Where are your manners, Ora?" Alec asked, smirking as he held my food just out of reach.

"May I please have my breakfast?" I asked, unenthused with his games. He leaned back and handed me my food. I thanked him and rolled my eyes. Alec started working here around the time I turned eighteen. He was an overweight pig who would sit in his chair staring at me. To say he made me uncomfortable was an understatement. He was currently watching me through the bars with a smile that revealed his thoughts. The door opened again, and I sighed with relief.

"Alec, for the hundredth time, leave this girl alone," Lonso scolded as he walked in seeing his face. To be emotionless about it, Lonso was my guard. They stuck all six foot five of this burly man with me the night I arrived, scared and snotty nosed. He handed me a tissue, smiled, and told me it would be okay. I was scared out of my mind the first night, crying the entire time. He brought my bed beside his desk and tucked me in so I could sleep while he worked. They let me sleep outside of the cell for a while but eventually made me return to it. Not long after, he would start bringing me things to make it more of a room than a cell. But no matter what he brought, it never made the bars disappear.

"I didn't even do anything." He feigned innocence, looking up at Lonso. He looked back at me, winking.

"You should have been upstairs already. You were supposed to give her the food and return to your post. Now go before I report you, again," Lonso threatened as he pulled him up from his chair. Alec frowned and quickly walked away. I smiled over at Alonso and rested my head against the bars.

"My hero."

"Anytime." He winked and leaned back in his chair. "Your hair is a mess."

"Well, you have been MIA these past couple of weeks. Where were you?" I asked.

"There was a death in the family. My godson's mother died. Poor kid. I had to go to the funeral and pick him up to come live with me." He ran a hand across his freckled face.

"I'm sorry."

"It's okay. She was a wonderful lady and lived a full life. I just feel bad for poor Luca. Mom is dead, and God knows his dad is out of the picture." He stood and grabbed an extra cup. "But he's strong. We'll get through this." He sat the cup on the platform and poured coffee from his thermos and handed it to me. I thanked him and took a sip. I felt bad for them both. I grew up hearing stories about his adventures with his friend Kya—about how much of a prankster she was, all of the fights they would get into together. I reached over and placed my hand on his. He gave me a small smile and patted my hand.

"I'm still trying, Ora. I haven't forgotten my promise," he told me, changing the subject. I took another sip of my coffee.

"Lonso…"

"They can't keep you in here forever." He turned to fully face me. "I've been putting money on your account for your release."

"You didn't have to do that." I shook my head. I couldn't imagine how much of his hard-earned money he'd put in my account for me.

"Ora, you know I love you like you're my own. It's not right for them to keep you in here for so long. Do you even remember what the outside world looks like?" he asked. Truthfully, I didn't. All I knew was what I could see from my small window above my bed and the bits I got in my dreams. I used to stand on my tiptoes just to stare at the sky. Those puffy white clouds reminded me of the cotton candy Lonso would sneak and give to me as a child.

"I want you to have a life. A real life. You need to be around people your own age and not just around a bunch of old guys and Peto." Peto hissed in his case, and I went to get him out. I placed him around my neck and went back over to the door. After Mr. Rat died, I was so messed up that I cried for days. Lonso felt bad and got me Peto. Snakes live a lot longer than rats, he told me. Peto was a four-lined snake and only a year old, and I loved him dearly. He is a wonderful judge of character and my most loyal friend aside from Lonso.

"Hey, Peto is a great conversationalist," I said as I kissed his head.

"I'm sure he is, but you need someone your age. That's why I want you to meet Luca." I raised an eyebrow. "I'll bring him by one of these days so you can meet him." I nodded quietly as I played with Peto. "I'll be back later to do your hair." He screwed the cap back onto his thermos and tucked it under his arm.

"Bye, baby girl."

"Bye, Lonso." He walked out the door and, with the thud of the door, left me alone.

My only connection to the outside world relies on my night-mares and Lonso's memory. In my dreams, it was always the same scenery—a dark forest glowing with the phosphorus of plants. My mother and I had on a deep shade of blue and a pair of flower crowns we'd made earlier that day. Her curls twisted and coiled between the flowers as if it was a part of her hair. My own was in a simple braid that a guard used to pull me from her arms. Screaming, we clawed at the lush grass of the forest floor, but our hands seemed to hold to nothing. My mother fought. She kicked a guard in the groin and pushed another one up against a willow tree. The third guard finally tied her hands behind her back and dragged her by her arms.

Lonso's outside world was a lot different. There weren't any glowing trees or thick vegetation but more buildings and snow, and it was cold. He would tell me of all the things you would see in the win-ter. Like the snow-covered mountains, trees dusted with snow from a storm. About how the hills looked like clouds. He once brought some snow to me just to prove that he wasn't lying about it. He placed some in my hand, and I immediately dropped it, shocked by the cold. He laughed and said, "I told you so." I sat and watched as the snow melted into a puddle that afternoon. I'd cried when there was no snow left. He explained that it melted when it was warm, and if he got me more, it would just melt too. I pouted and he ran a hand over my hair. "You'll see it one day, little one."

That day never came.

Almost twelve years had passed since then, and I was still trapped. The only thing that kept me sane was Lonso and Peto, I thought, staring into my beautiful pet's eyes.

"We may never get out of here, Peto." He slithered and ran his head over my cheek. I smiled and leaned against the wall.

"Excuse me," said a male voice. I hadn't heard the door open, and yet here this man was. He was quite tall, his skin a deep red-dish-brown. But what caught me most was his glowing orange eyes that were encased with long lashes. A scar ran down his cheek just below his right eye as if he got lucky in a fight. He looked around awkwardly as I stared. He was the first guy I've ever seen close to my age.

"I'm sorry." I shook my head, failing to stop staring. I couldn't find the words so he spoke.

"Have you seen a man named Alonso?" he spoke differently, but then again, I only knew three people.

I nodded. "He left not too long ago. I don't know where he is, though."

"Right"—he stared at me for a bit more—"do you know when he'll be back?"

"Probably not for a few more hours. He usually comes down to have dinner with me." He let out a sigh and plopped down in the chair. We sat in silence for a while, him looking down at his hands and me playing with Peto. I stole glances at him, still wondering who this person was. He had pictures on his arms that ran all the way down to his wrist that was circled by a small woven bracelet. I'd begun to think he'd fallen asleep, but he eventually sat up and turned to look at me.

"So what did you do?"

"Sorry?"

"What did you do to end up in here?" My brow furrowed, and I shook my head. "Sorry, I was just—" he started, realizing he offended me.

"I didn't do anything," I replied, cutting him off. His expression changed.

"Well, you must have if…"

"I didn't do anything," I repeated curtly. He raised his hands and said nothing more.

After a moment, I spoke, "I've been here as long as I can remember." I looked over and saw his face soften in compassion. "Someone took me away from my mother as a child and brought me here."

"I'm sorry," he said quietly. I shrugged. I didn't bother telling him about how much money needed to be paid in order for me to be set free. It was more than anyone ever had imagined. And yet Lonso has been trying to pay it bit by bit all these years.

"I kind of know how it feels. For your mom to be out of your life." I turned from where I was sitting to face him. "My mom just died recently."

"I'm sorry." I could only imagine how he felt, and suddenly, it struck me. "Oh, you must be Luca."

"I am." He pulled his chair closer to the bars. "And you must be Ora. Lonso has told me a lot about you." He reached his hand through, and I shook it. Peto crawled from my hand onto his arm. "And who is this?"

"His name is Peto." He smiled as he held him, and Peto slithered up his arm in happiness. Luca must be a good person because Peto tends to bite those he doesn't like.

I sat directly in front of him with my legs crossed. "How did you end up with Peto?"

"Lonso gave him to me a couple of years ago. It took him a while to give me another pet after Mr. Rat died."

Luca snorted. "Sounds about right. He used to drive my mom crazy with all the animals he'd bring home for me."

I watched him for a moment as he played with Peto. He was a big guy, but I appreciated how gentle he was with him. His sadness seemed to subside for a bit. I heard the door open and looked up.

"Ah, so you've met Luca," Lonso greeted with a big smile.

"I have." Luca passed Peto to me, then stood to hug his godfather. They hugged for a moment, and I watched as Lonso held him by the neck. I felt so bad for him. For a moment, you could see Luca's frame shake as if he was crying.

"She told me you would be coming back, so I just decided to wait here," he told him, pulling away.

"Smart decision," Lonso replied, nodding. "I'd hate for you to get lost in this place." As he spoke, I took a moment to look around. I'd never really noticed how shabby this place was. Lonso had always made it feel fun and didn't let my attention wander to the bad side. Now that I'm older and looking at it, I began to notice how small everything was. How my mattress was only a few steps from my sink and toilet. I'm sure if I lay down, I'd only have a few inches before my feet touched the other end. At least it was slightly bigger from wall to gate.

"I decided to come back early so I could do your hair as promised." I smiled as he unlocked my gate and patted the chair in front of him. As he did my hair, we all talked, and honestly, it was amazing. I learned that Luca was an only child. He had a twin brother who unfortunately died when they were younger in some freak accident. When Lonso mentioned it to me, I could see Luca's body go stiff. Lonso glanced at him and quickly changed the subject. He was quiet for a while after that but seemed to open up more when I asked him about where he was from.

"Argo is honestly the most beautiful place on earth. It's full of lush trees that reach the sky and birds the size of children. There are a lot of volcanoes, but they never reach the areas where people live. It has mountains covered with trees and waterfalls and…well, you'd have to see it to get the full picture," he said, his face lighting up.

"It sounds beautiful. I wish I could see it."

Luca smiled and looked down at his hands. "And one day you will. I promise." Lonso patted my shoulders before going back to my hair.

After a while, another guard came to drop off my dinner as he finished the last lock. He wiped his hands on a cloth and stood back. "I am so good at that."

I laughed and thanked him with a hug. He left and quickly returned with enough food for him and Luca. As we ate our dinner, Lonso kept things light by telling us stories about his childhood.

"I remember this one time when we were kids, Kya and I were at the beach and she tried to drown me." He laughed, almost choking on his food.

"How is that funny?' Luca questioned, looking confused.

"She did it because she was upset because I had buried her stuff in the sand. It took her hours to find it all," he told us roaring in laughter. We busted out laughing, almost falling out of our seats.

It was honestly the best night of my life.

*****

A few months passed since I met Luca, and I haven't seen him since. Lonso would give me brief updates but wouldn't go much into detail. Something about how he was needed at home. I enjoyed his company the night we met, but now I started to think that maybe he just did not enjoy me as much as I did him. Perhaps that was why he stayed away for so long. Days began to blend together, and I eventually lost track. I'd spend my days dreaming about the Argo that Luca described. I pictured myself climbing to the tops of mountains and finding where all the birds slept at night. I could feel a warm breeze on my face, the sun radiating on my skin. The longer I lay there, the more it felt like I was there. The only problem was that I wasn't. I was stuck in this small space that had been my home for the majority of my life. The walls were colorless concrete that seemed to make the room seem smaller. The floors were stone that never seemed clean. The only light was a large one that hung from the ceiling in the middle of the room. The only decoration was drawings I'd taped to the walls over the years—mostly pictures of animals that Lonso would describe to me or places he'd been. I pulled my knees to my chest and cradled Peto in my arms. I'd never felt so alone.

"Hey," Luca said as he came through the door. I glanced at him and back at Peto.

"Hi," I responded, trying to hide my excitement. He was wearing all black today, creating a blank canvas for his eyes to shine.

"How are you?" He sat down on the floor across from me.

"I've been better," I replied with a shrug.

He nodded. "Come here, I want to show you something."

I padded over and sat across from him. He smiled and slid a piece of paper under the bar to me. I picked it up and gasped.

"Did you draw this?"

"Yeah, do you like it?" he asked with pride.

I nodded as I admired the picture. There were tall trees thick with leaves, a waterfall that poured into a river, and mountains in the background. It was exactly how I imagined it.

"Is this Argo?" I asked, looking up finally.

"It is." He smiled. "I thought it would help you visualize."

"It's exactly how I envisioned it." I stared at the picture a little bit longer. It was so beautiful.

"My mother used to take me on a trail through the forest, and we'd have lunch at the bottom of a volcano." He looked down at his hands, remembering.

"What was she like?" I rested my head on my hand.

"She was amazing." He sniffled. "She had skin the color of honey and these big orange eyes. She was so sweet, always feeding and taking care of people. She had this, this fire in her. I can't explain it. Everyone looked up to her in our village. She was so easy to talk to. I could tell her anything, and she'd always know what to say, even if I didn't want to hear it. I just really miss her." A small tear escaped his eyes, and he quickly wiped it away. I reached between the bars and grabbed his hand.

"I miss my mom too."

There wasn't much else I could say. I'd never experienced the kind of mom he had. My own mom was loving and cared for me, but I was too young to remember any of the important stuff, the things that would get me through days without her. I guess not knowing her is both a blessing and a curse. You can't really miss what you do not know.

"Do you remember anything about your mom?"

"Not really. I just have flashes of her in my dreams. From what I can remember, she looks a lot like me. The only difference is her hair." I sometimes wondered if we had the same personality too.

We didn't speak for a while. I'd eventually retracted my hand, feeling too awkward to leave it there. I stood to tape his drawing above my bed where I could see it. He commented on some of my animal drawings and even tried to hide his laughter at what must have been a horrible interpretation of those animals. As we talked, I found myself staring at him once again. His coily hair was shaved on the sides and tall at the top, each coil seeming to dance with another. His eyes were a brownish orange in the dim light and dulled by the sadness behind them. His hands were quite large and encased a few golden rings with intricate designs. My eyes trailed up to the pictures on his arms.

"Tribal tattoos," he explained. I leaned in closer as he held his arm out for me to look.

"They're ink drawings on your skin. This one is a dragon, my village symbol." I watched as he rotated his arm to better display the majestic creature. I asked what a dragon was, and he gladly explained. I'd never heard of a large birdlike creature that breathes fire. He laughed at the shocked look on my face.

"I want a tattoo," I made known. I loved the idea of having your art wherever you go. "I want one of the moon and the night sky on my arm."

"I'll bring my stuff and give you one next time," he promised. I smiled at the thought of him coming back. Perhaps I had a friend after all.

*****

He'd come back as promised with a small case and Lonso in tow. He let me out so that Luca could have a better angle for his work. He pulled out a long thin needle and dipped it in a black liquid and looked up at me.

"This might hurt," he warned. I turned my arm ever so slightly away, and he laughed. "You have to be still for this to work." I bit my lip and nodded. Keeping his eyes on mine, he placed the needle over my skin and I flinched, making my arm jolt.

"Ora," he sighed.

"I'm sorry," I apologized, putting my arm back where it was.

The first poke wasn't so bad. It was all of the other ones that really hurt. I tried looking at Lonso for something to distract me, but he just sat there watching and smirking at each wince. I looked over at Peto, my only sympathizer. He had designs all along his body, but they were there from birth. Lucky.

"How long does this usually take?" I questioned anxiously. Lonso laughed and told me to relax as he handed me a glass of water. I sipped it slowly, wishing the water would make its way to my arm and numb the pain.

"It won't take much longer," Luca reassured. I stared over at the picture he gave me, then closed my eyes, imagining that I was walking through the trees and the pain was just leaves and branches scratching me as I walked along the trail.

"Done," Luca confirmed as he sat back to admire his work. I twisted my arm and gasped. It was exactly what I wanted—a full moon surrounded by dark clouds and stars.

"I love it! Thank you!" I leaned over and hugged him.

"You're welcome." He laughed as he hugged me back.

"Well, isn't that cute." Luca shot a look at Lonso who winked back at him.

"You have to be careful. Don't mess up the tattoo," he informed me as he put his kit away.

We hung out for a bit before he had to go. I was sad to see him leave, but he promised he would come back tomorrow.

And he did. He came back day after day as promised. With each visit, he would tell me about different places he'd been, bringing me different foods to try and draw more pictures for me. He was patient when I asked him questions and seemed willing to explain something I didn't get the first time. I began to look forward to his visits and sometimes found myself watching the door waiting for him to arrive. Lonso was always nearby smirking in the corner somewhere, as if he knew something I didn't.

One day as Luca was telling me a story about birds, he stopped and stared at me quizzically.

"You have freckles," he stated.

"Freckles?"

He pointed to my face. "The black dots on your nose and cheeks. I guess this lighting is so bad I never noticed before." I got up from where I was sitting and looked closely in the mirror. Touching my face with a wet rag, I realized they were indeed freckles as he said and not smudges I could wipe off. I ran my hands over my cheeks checking out the little black dots. I'd never noticed them before. I went back to where I was sitting and looked at him.

"How do I get them off?"

"You don't." He laughed but stopped when he saw my expression. "It's just something you have. The same way having violet eyes is just something you have." I sat there and contemplated if I even wanted freckles.

"Don't worry, you're still pretty with them," he complimented. I blushed and thanked him, looking down. He nodded before going back to telling me his story.

"Dragons are these beautiful winged creatures that blow fire from their mouths. They're usually mild tempered unless threatened, but otherwise, they're very gentle animals." He told me about how big their wings were and how high they can fly. He even drew me a breathtaking picture so I could better imagine what he was describing.

Lonso coughed loudly for a moment, disrupting my thoughts. We both looked over at him as he wheezed, trying to catch his breath. Luca ran over and patted his back.

"I'm okay." He waved him away as he grabbed his water. Luca reluctantly came and sat back down. We stared at him for a moment, just making sure he was okay.

*****

But of course, he wasn't. His cough got worse and worse as time went by. It started as just a cough and slowly developed into a body-shaking hack. He always seemed out of breath and wheezed with each step he took. Luca and I were starting to get concerned.

"Lonso, I think you should go see a doctor," I suggested for the hundredth time.

"I don't believe in doctors," he asserted.

Luca rolled his eyes. "Well, they exist, and you need to go see one. We're worried about you." I nodded, backing him up.

"Okay, I hear you guys." He let out a heavy sigh. "I'll go see one."

Luca turned and gave me a reassuring smile as if to say he would make sure he goes. Relieved, I gave him a small smile and touched his shoulder. I knew he would watch over him where I couldn't. Lonso eventually left to do some office work, and once he was gone, Luca turned to me.

"I'll take him in the morning. He's always been skeptical about anything doctor related."

I could understand his dislike of doctors. I'd hated seeing them as a child. "Do you think it's anything serious?"

"I hope not, but it's best we go see one just in case."

That night, as I lay in my bed, I couldn't help but think about Lonso. I honestly didn't know what I would do if something happened to him. I don't know what Luca would do either. He'd finally started to be able to talk about his mom without getting choked up. I feel like if Lonso were to die too… I shook the thought out of my head. *No, he would be okay*, I told myself as I drifted off to sleep.

The next morning, I woke up earlier than usual. I hadn't slept much because I kept tossing and turning all night, worried about Lonso. I sat there and played with Peto as I watched the sky turn from the reds and golds of morning to the bright blue of day. Peto slithered up my arm and into my shirt. I laughed at the light tickle against my skin. He always made me feel better when I was down.

"Ora." I looked up smiling at Luca, but it fell when I saw the sad look on his face.

"What happened? Is he okay?" I rushed over to the bar.

"The doctor says there isn't much he can do for him. That his breathing is getting worse, something to do with his lungs." He shook his head. He came so close to the bar I could see the sadness in his eyes, the breaking of his heart.

"So what does that mean? He'll be okay, right?"

"I don't know," he admitted quietly. He leaned his forehead against the cold bars and closed his eyes. I reached through and touched his cheek. He let out a heavy sigh but didn't open his eyes. *Please be okay, Lonso. What are we going to do without you? Who would talk to me and teach me about the outside world? Who would lock my hair? Who would I tell all of my secrets to?* And poor Luca. Lonso was the only family he had left. What would happen to him if he died? I felt bad, but I can only imagine the feeling of immense pain of having no one to turn to. A small tear ran down my cheek, and Luca gently wiped it away.

"Don't cry." I opened my eyes and stared into his. Despite how bleak the situation was, staring in those auburn eyes, I knew whatever would happen, we'd be okay. I just didn't know how yet.

A thought suddenly struck me. What if something did happen and Luca stopped coming around too? What would I do? Completely alone without Lonso or Luca to make my existence in this place bearable, where would that leave me? I couldn't live here much longer without Lonso; he was the only person that I could talk to. Without him, I was left with creepy guards and the slow rhythmic drip of water from the ceiling. I backed away from the gate, no need to keep getting attached to someone I'd just end up losing too.

"Ora, what's wrong?" I shook my head and went to sit back on the bed. "Ora."

"You're going to leave me too," I whispered.

"What makes you say that?"

"If something happens to Lonso, you'll stop coming around. Then I'll be alone, again," I admitted.

"That's not true," he reassured.

"Yes, it is," I replied quietly.

"It's not, and you know why?" I looked up at him. "Because I care about you. I'd never leave you, at least not on purpose." He smirked. I laughed, then sighed in defeat. "Come here."

I walked back to the gate in front of him, and he reached through and gave me a hug.

"You're my best friend, Ora, I'd never leave you." I rested my head against the bars and let the tears flow. "Now stop crying." I smiled and swiped them away.

"I wish I could leave this place."

"And you will. I'll do everything I can to get you out of here. Lonso too." Somehow I believed him this time.

A few weeks went by, and Luca always came back as promised, but I began to see less and less of Lonso. The first time, he seemed fine, aside from the occasional cough. He was acting normal, laughing, talking, and even cracking jokes. His high spirits seemed to dwindle as the weeks passed by. He eventually got so bad that he struggled just to open the door. It saddened my heart to see him like that. And one, day he didn't come back, and neither did Luca.

My mind began to wander to the worst-case scenario, and as the days went by, I became more convinced. I tried not to harbor bitter feelings for Luca; he must be going through a lot, but I couldn't help but feel abandoned.

"I guess it's just you and me, Peto." I wrapped him around my neck and leaned my head against the wall.

*****

"Wake up!" I grumbled at the voice that disturbed my already lacking sleep. I threw the blanket over my head. Alec began clacking his coffee cup against the bars.

"What do you want?" I yelled.

"Your debt has been paid," he mumbled before taking a long sip. I flipped the cover back from over my head.

"What did you say?"

"Your debts have been paid. You're free," he stated as he unlocked my door and went out of the room. I sat with my mouth open, sheets rumpled around me, and stared at the door. I cautiously got out of bed, looking around. This can't be right, could it? I pulled on my sweater and walked to the door. I took one hesitant step after the other while watching the door. It suddenly burst open, and I ran back to my bed.

"Luca?" He walked in, looking flustered right over to me.

"How did your door get open?" he questioned, looking around.

"Why do you care?" I snapped. I was beyond upset. I hadn't seen him in over a month. So much for promises. He took a step closer as I moved away.

"Ora…"

"No. You left me after you promised that you wouldn't." I moved around him to the other side of the cell.

"I didn't leave you, Ora. I—"

"So what do you call you not showing up for weeks on end then?" I cut him off.

"It wasn't on purpose, I couldn't come—"

"And why not?" my voice raised. I didn't want to hear his excuses.

"Because Lonso was dying!" he screamed. My folded arms dropped to my sides. He walked over to my bed and sat down and ran his hands over his already drained face. My anger instantly faded as I went to sit next to him.

"We thought he was getting better, but then he got sick. It eventually got to the point where he was bedridden and I had to take care of everything for him. He told me to go see you, but I was too afraid something would happen to him while I was gone," he confessed.

"So where is he now?" I whispered. But of course I knew. "When did it happen?"

"Last night. I came here to do something for him."

"What?"

"He wanted me to pay the rest of your debt."

CHAPTER

"He did what?"

"He only had one payment left on your debt. He was going to surprise you and pay for it, but he…couldn't," he told me, his voice cracking.

You won't be here forever, Ora, I promise. Those words rang in my ears. I couldn't believe that even with his dying breath, he wanted to make sure I was okay. I sniffled back the tears as Luca threw an arm around my shoulders.

"Can I go see him?"

He shook his head. "The funeral was yesterday. I'm sorry, Ora." I took one shaky breath and nodded.

"No, it's okay, I understand." I looked up at the ceiling. I hope he knew in those last moments how much I loved him.

"He wanted me to give you this," Luca replied, handing me a piece of paper.

> *Dear Ora,*
>
> *I never thought this day would come, but I guess I was a fool to think I would live forever. I love you, Ora. You were the daughter I always wanted, and I cherished every moment with you. Despite your bleak circumstances, you never let that affect you, and I want you to never let it. You are an amazing young lady with so much to offer.*

I always promised I'd get you out, and now I have. I want you to go explore the world and learn along the way. It is more beautiful than I could ever describe to you.
I love you.

Lonso

My tears stained the pages and blurred my vision. I carefully folded it back and held it to my chest. I would keep this letter for the rest of my life. Luca reached up and wiped the tears from my cheeks and slowly dragged it off my cheeks. His long lashes were damp with tears that sparkled in the light. He ran a thumb over my cheek, then leaned his forehead against mine. I took a deep breath and leaned in, closing my eyes.

"Come with me." I opened my eyes and stared back at him.

"You want me to come with you? But to where?"

"Back to Argo." He leaned away and looked at me. "I wouldn't just leave you here. Now that Lonso is gone, I have to take care of you." My face fell.

"Oh."

"It's not like that. He didn't make me. I want you to come with me. You're my best friend," he clarified. "The only one, really." He was my only friend too.

I wasn't just hesitant about leaving with him; I was hesitant about leaving. I didn't know anything about the world outside. All I've ever known were these four walls—the drafty windows that let in bone-chilling air in the winter, the leaky ceiling that dripped rhythmically, and the dim lights. Lonso and this cell was all I've ever known, and the idea of even stepping outside terrified me. I didn't have anything or anyone except for Luca. I was so lost in my head that I didn't notice when Luca got up. I watched him pull items of clothing from my bins and put them into a black bag. He grabbed my toiletries and placed them into the bag, then turned to face me. He held out his hand, and I took it gratefully.

"Is this all of your stuff?" he asked, already knowing the answer. I stood and walked over to Peto's cage. I picked him up and placed him around my neck. I then grabbed my wool blanket, wrapping it around my shoulders. "Ready to go?" I gave a hesitant nod. He tightened his grip on my hand and led me through the door.

*****

I stood hesitantly in the doorway, afraid to take another step. We managed to get through the building fairly quickly. He paused in front of a huge iron door with ring handles. He grabbed one of the rings and pulled it toward himself. The door groaned and creaked as he pulled it open. Wind rushed through and blew my hair from my shoulders. I squinted in the glaring light and took a deep breath. *Mmm, fresh air.* I'd become so accustomed to the air in my cell that the deep breath I took made me cough. Luca walked through the open door and turned around to face me. I stared at my feet, which seemed incapable of moving.

"Ora," he called. I looked up, and my breath caught. He was even more handsome in the sunlight, and what was even more beautiful was the landscape behind him. The sun was high in the sky, burning yellow and bright, while big fluffy clouds floated around it. There were trees of all shapes and sizes, and hills that rose and fell. Flowers were sprinkled throughout the trees and dotted along the pathway that ended in front of the doorway I stood petrified behind.

"Just one step, Ora," Luca said with an outstretched hand. I grabbed his hand, and he slowly pulled me through the doorway. I stepped into the soft grass and wiggled my toes. It was everything I imagined. "Are you okay?"

"Yes," I replied, smiling. He smiled back and threw my bag over his shoulder with his other hand. He led me along the trail, walking slowly so I could admire everything I saw. The flowers were different shapes and sizes and colors and yet were all so beautiful. Luca reached down, grabbed one, and tucked it behind my ear. I blushed as I reached up and felt the blooming flower. I looked at the ground as we walked, admiring all the little animals. "Bugs?" I think Lonso said. They trailed one after another in an assembly line. I watched as they walked from one end of the path to another before disappearing into the grass. Everything must seem so big to them. My head shot up to the sound of birds. I stopped in my tracks as I watched two birds fly around each other while singing. I loved songbirds. They were the only animals that ever came to my tiny cell window. They would sometimes wake me up with their songs, but it never bothered me. I thought they were singing especially for me, trying to lift my mood. Luca turned when he realized I had stopped and looked up to see what I was staring at.

"Oh nice, you found some starlings."

"Starlings?" What a pretty name for the bird.

He nodded. "At first glance they look like crows, but if you look closely, their feathers are like rainbows in the light." I stared in awe as I noticed their feathers. They were beautiful shades of blues, purples, and greens.

"I know it's a lot to take in all at once, but we have a long way to go before it gets dark. So we have to keep moving," he told me apologetically. I apologized, and we started walking again.

*****

We eventually stopped in a small village around sunset. We'd been walking since that morning, and needless to say, we were exhausted. Tall trees stood around the entrance like a nature-made gate. A little sign that read "Verdea" peeked through. My eyes glowed in the light from the burning lanterns that hung in front of homes and shops. Every building looked the same except for a sign or two to identify what each place was. The roads were made of stone and felt hard under my thin shoes. In the lowering sun, I could see that the village was surrounded by hills. The hills loomed over the town as if they were in the center of a bowl. The villagers stared as we walked through the streets, clearly noting that we were outsiders. They all looked different except for their eyes, which were a deep green that reminded me of the grass.

Luca grabbed my hand and led me into a shop and to a small table. He explained that it was a restaurant, a place where you could get food. As we sat, a woman walked up to us with a smile. She sat two glasses of water on the table before rambling on about some food that was being served for dinner.

"That's fine," Luca replied. The young woman smiled, bobbing her head. She stared at Luca for a beat and then walked away. She was clearly attracted to him. I couldn't blame her. Those eyes and his tall muscular build were enough to make any girl swoon. She quickly returned with our bowls and placed a basket of bread on the table.

"Can I get you anything else?" she asked Luca as she played with her hair.

"No, thank you." He reached for some bread and broke it in half before handing it to me. The woman frowned and walked away. I took a bite out of my bread, smirking. Luca shook his head and dipped his bread in his bowl before taking a bite.

"So what is this?" I asked curiously as I stared into my bowl.

"Beef stew. It's just meat and vegetables basically. Try it, it's good." I took a spoonful and was surprised by the taste. I chewed and sighed. "See, I told you." He smiled. As we ate, I began to think about our journey again.

"So what's next?"

"Well, we'll stay here for tonight and then we will leave first thing in the morning. Argo isn't too far from here," he told me in-between bites of food. I didn't know where we would sleep, but I'm sure he had that figured out already. I looked around the restaurant and saw all of the villagers sitting and having their dinner. Two big guys occupied a corner where they were loudly playing cards. They stood up in each other's faces as they accused each other of cheating. A couple was juggling eating and cleaning up after their small children who were throwing and spilling food everywhere. Another couple sat more toward the door, holding hands as they partook in what appeared to be a deep conversation.

"Are you done?" Luca asked before eating the last of the bread. I nodded, and he reached into his pocket and threw some coins on the table. We stood and walked back out onto the street. After a short stroll, we eventually stopped at a booth.

"Ah yes, how may I help you?" a short man asked behind the booth. He had big puffy cheeks and a red beard that covered the bottom half of his face.

"We would like a room for tonight," Luca asked.

"That will be ten shingles." Luca handed him the money. The man bent to write something down before he came from behind the booth and led us into the building behind him. We walked up the stairs behind him, stopping so he could unlock a door. He opened the door and held it open for us to walk in. The room was lit up by a small lamp that sat on a table by the bed. There was a big fuzzy rug the shade of blood in the middle of the floor. In the corner was a desk and a chair and a wide dresser. Two windows framed the wall the bed was against. They were big enough that I could see the street down below and the night sky. I walked over to the window and stared down at the villagers. Everyone was packing up for the night, trying to make their way home. I turned and saw Luca plopping our bags onto the dresser, dropping the keys beside them. The man closed the door behind us, leaving us in silence. Luca held open the door by the small table, showing me that it was a bathroom before walking in to use it. A thought crossed my mind as I listened to the water run. He walked back in wiping his wet face off with a towel.

"Luca?" He looked up at me. "Where is the other bed?"

"Oh. Uh, I can sleep on the floor," he offered.

"No, it's okay." It would be awkward, but just from walking on that rug, I could tell it was hard and itchy. He gave a short nod before motioning me toward the door. He showed me how to work the shower and gave me a towel and a washcloth before he left the room. It was filled with steam that left a thin layer of water over everything. I turned the knob on the right and jumped back before the water caught me. Stepping in, I sighed as the hot water rolled off my skin. Showers were indeed heavenly. For so many years, I'd just used a washcloth and the sink water to clean myself. The water was steady, but it was never hot. This, now this was way better. I stood under the water for a moment, then cleaned myself, struggling to pull myself from the water. Thankfully, Luca left my night clothes here. I blushed at the thought of having to walk past him and get them. I quickly dried off and pulled on my nightshirt and shorts. I took deep breaths as I put my hair up for the night. *It'll be fine,* I reassured myself. I opened the door and dropped my towel. My eyes trailed up every muscle as I stared at the back of his head. He was shirtless, only wearing pajama shorts. I watched as his arms flexed as he reached down and put some clothes back in his bag. After a moment, he turned and smiled.

"How was your shower?" he asked, putting our clothes away.

I shook my head trying to clear it. "It was great." I quickly bent down to get my towel and walked to the table, folding it there.

"Awesome. So the plan is to leave after breakfast in the morning. It shouldn't take too long to get to Argo." I nodded, letting him know I was listening. "Once we get there, I'll introduce you to my family."

"Your family?"

"Yes, we'll be living with them once we're there. Don't worry, they're all nice," he added once he saw my expression.

"Can't wait." I sat on the bed and leaned my head against the wall. I quickly jumped up realizing I had forgotten to take Peto out of his carrier once we got to the room. I wrapped him around my neck, apologizing, before getting out his food to feed him. Once he was done, I placed him on the coat rack hoping he would enjoy the space.

"Did you want a specific side?" Luca asked, motioning to the bed.

"Uhm, the left is fine." I never did like sleeping next to the door. I'd sleep with my feet toward the gate just in case. I walked over to the bed and slowly sat down.

"I'm not going to try anything, promise." I lay down facing the wall. He lay down and reached for the lamp. "Good night."

And with a click, we were thrown into quiet and darkness. Through my shirt, I could feel his warm back against mine, burning a hole through the fabric. I tried to clear my mind and think of calmer things so I could sleep. I pulled the covers up over my shoulders and closed my eyes.

*****

I panted harder and harder as my chest began to burn from the intensity. My short legs tripped over a vine and scrambled to the ground. I rushed to pick up my things in the dark phosphorous floor. I could hear the dogs close behind.

"Focus, Ora!" My mother yelled as she stood me up and pulled me deeper into the forest. Willows wisped around us as she moved them out of her way with one hand. The howls of the dogs seemed to get closer no matter how fast we ran. My mother squeezed my hand tighter as I began to cry, not bothering to stop and wipe my tears. A single dog ran above the pack, cutting us off. My mother pulled me behind her and stretched out her hand before the dog charged toward us.

*****

I bolted upright in bed feeling as if my heart was on fire. I struggled for a moment to catch my breath.

"Hey, are you okay?" he asked, rubbing his eyes. I nodded, hoping he could see me in the dark room. "Bad dream?"

"Something like that," I replied, wiping the sweat from my brow.

"Hey, come here." He held an outstretched arm on my side, and I gratefully lay on it. He stroked my arm with the other hand, assuring me that I was safe. Lying with my head crooked into the shadow of his neck, I started to believe him and closed my eyes.

*****

We woke up early the next morning. My eyes fluttered in the light of sunrise coming through the window. I yawned and rubbed my eyes as I watched Luca get up. He stood, stretching with a yawn before he padded over to the bathroom. After I heard a flush, I went into the bathroom to grab my toothbrush. Brushing my teeth next to him, I couldn't help but feel embarrassed as I remembered last night. I'd never slept beside anyone before.

"How did you sleep?"

30

"It was good, you?" Even as I replied, I hoped my face wouldn't give me away.

"Also good."

I left the bathroom once I was done, and he shut the door. I pulled out a pair of pants and a top and pulled my sweater on it. He emerged from the bathroom dressed and began gathering everything into our bags.

"We're going to get breakfast and then we will leave. We'll come back for the bags." He grabbed the keys from the small table and held the door open for me. After locking our room, we headed to the restaurant where we had dinner last night. Luca ordered for the both of us, and soon after, we got our food. There were eggs, toast, and some kind of meat.

"It's bacon," he told me laughing as my eyes darted toward him. "Go on, try it. It's good." I picked it up and took a bite. It was crunchy, salty, and very greasy but still good. I shrugged and continued eating. After he was finished, Luca stood and told me he was going to check out.

"Finish your food. I'll be right back," he promised. I nodded and continued eating.

"Hello." I slowly looked up to see a tall handsome man hovering over me.

"Hi," I said shyly. He smiled and sat across from me where Luca sat. He was rather slim and had short black hair. He had the same wide green eyes the other villagers had and a wide smile that revealed a set of white teeth.

"What is a guy like that doing with an omnikinetic like you?" he asked, smirking.

"A what?" What was an omnikinetic?

"Your eyes are purple," he mentioned as if that would explain what he was saying.

"I don't know what you're talking about," I told him, looking around.

"Well, nevertheless, you're far too beautiful to be left at a table alone," he replied, ignoring my comment. He stretched his hand across the table, and instinctively, I pulled mine away. He turned his arms palm up and squeezed it closed, then opened it. From his hand grew a beautiful glowing flower. My eyes widened in amazement as he plucked it from his palm and handed it to me. I spun the flower between my fingertips and admired its beauty. It reminded me of the flowers in my dreams.

"It's beautiful, thank you."

"You're welcome, my dear. Would you like to go on a date with me?"

"Uh, a date?"

"Yes. When are you leaving town?" he eagerly asked.

"We're leaving now," Luca replied for me as he slapped a hand on his shoulder, making him jump.

"Look," I said, showing him the flower he gave me. He smiled then continued glaring at the man.

"I believe you are in my seat," he told him low in his ear. The man pressed his lips together and nodded vigorously before getting up. Luca placed our bags at his feet and folded his hands, waiting for him to leave. The man's eyes darted from him to mine and back before quickly walking away. "What a nuisance." I couldn't help but laugh.

"He looked so scared." I laughed.

"He should've been. What did he say to you?" he asked.

"He kept calling me beautiful. Then he made me this flower and asked me out," I replied, toying with my flower. Luca scoffed and grabbed our bags from the floor.

"Of course, he did. It's time to get going." I stood and took one of my bags from him, carefully tucking my flower in the side pocket. He shook his head and led me out the door.

Hours had passed since we left the restaurant, and it seemed as if we were going in circles. The path looked the same since we started walking, but Luca insisted he knew where we were.

"You never forget how to get back home," he told me as I began to ask questions. We eventually stopped to eat lunch, which was some bread and cheese he picked up in Verdea. It had warmed from the trip but was still filling. I sat munching on the slightly mushy cheese as I looked around. Just in the distance, I could see where the trees cleared and a long plain stretched to meet between two mountains.

"It's right there," he said between mouthfuls of food, "at the bottom of those volcanoes."

"Volcanoes?" My eyes widened. I remember being confused when Lonso tried to explain to me as a child that there were huge mountains that spouted fiery liquid called lava. "Aren't those dangerous?"

"They're dormant. They're not expected to erupt anytime soon. Perfectly safe." I nodded looking at the volcanoes in the distance. I took a swig out of my water canteen, then wiped my mouth with the back of my hand. He popped his last piece of bread in his mouth, then stood, wiping his hands on his pants. I stood and stretched my limbs. Grabbing our things, we started our way back through the path.

When we finally reached the clearing, I stood in awe. Tucked just behind a curtain of willow leaves was a beautiful land. There were tall fruit trees that stood high above houses made of straw and leaves. These huge huts were decorated with giant leaves and flowers that adorned doorways and the edge of the roof. The grass was a thick green, and bushes lined the village's sides as if it were forming a fence. Large rocks were scattered throughout, but in the center was an impressive rock sculpture that surrounded a statue of an animal. I made a mental note to get a closer look at it later.

The women wore grass skirts and shirts made of intertwined leaves and vine. Beads were wrapped around their bare waists as well as their ankles that jingled with each step. The men wore skirts made of a beautiful fabric and no shirt. Their bare chests instead were covered with tattoos, each one different from the next. They were all different shades of a warm brown but had the same alluring eyes as Luca.

As we stepped further into the village, a group of elderly women dropped their weaving and ran over to us.

"Luca!" they called excitedly in unison. They trapped him in a massive bear hug and kissed him all over his face.

"Ulikuwa wapi [Where were you]?" one of the grandmothers scolded as she popped him in the arm.

"Lonso alikufa [Lonso died]." Her expression softened, and she pulled his head to her chest. He hugged her back tightly, allowing her big arms to wrap around his tall frame.

"Tulisika juu ya kile kilichotokea. Alikuwa mtu mzuri, lakini itakuwa sawa asali. Ninaahidi [We heard about what happened. He was a good man, but it'll be okay honey. I promise]." She kissed his temple and looked over my way. "Who is this beautiful girl with you?" I gave a shy smile, and she motioned me forward. I walked over, and the group of ladies began examining me.

"She is quite beautiful."

"Not too skinny too *mhm*. That's good."

Luca laughed and began introducing them to me. Tegan was the plump grandmother who had wrapped her arms around Luca. She had skin the color of honey and big orange eyes framed by thick lashes. Her hair was tied up in a messy bun with curls spilling out. Esther, however, looked more like Luca with her bright eyes and dark skin. She had locks like mine and a playful smile adorned with purple lipstick. Amla hadn't spoken aside from her greeting. I could tell she wasn't much for words, but she had a warm smile and knowing eyes that spoke for her.

"You must be hungry," Esther stated as she touched my locks, smiling. "I have a special concoction for your hair. Remind me to give it to you later." I nodded as she smiled and looped her arm through mine. Tegan and Amla grabbed Luca and began walking with me and Esther towing behind.

"Where are you from, my dear?" she asked politely as we strolled along the path.

"I'm not sure actually," I replied, trying to figure out the best way to answer her question without telling her my life story.

Her brow furrowed. "Well, that's unfortunate." She was silent for a moment before she spoke. She asked about how I met Luca, and I told her about how close I was to Alonso and how he had introduced us.

"*Aibu gani*. What a shame. He was such a good man." She shook her head. "He was like a father to poor Luca, especially after his mother passed. We all have to take extra care of him now that Lonso is gone," she expressed to me with a serious look. I gave her a firm nod understanding what she meant. She was counting on me to watch over him.

As we walked, she pointed out different places and told me what they were. She described all of the plants, animals, and even some history about Argo. The village was picturesque with its lush grass and tall fruit and nut trees. Flowers grew around the houses and along dirt paths that lead every which way. I stood in awe the further we walked into the village. There was just so much life to everyone—from the kids running around playing together to the grandmothers and mothers weaving baskets and collecting wood. My eyes lingered over a woman who was braiding her daughter's hair between her legs. I swallowed the lump in my throat and looked away.

We stopped walking when we reached a fairly large hut and ducked inside. I was instructed to take my shoes off at the door. I kicked them off, then sat on the floor next to Esther. The others gathered around and formed a circle.

"I know you are tired from your travels, but there are things we must discuss, Luca," Tegan expressed as she looked at him. He nodded as he continued to look down. Amla grabbed a bowl of fruit and placed it in the middle, motioning for me to take some. I smiled and grabbed a fruit I'd never seen before. I sniffed it and brought it to my mouth before Esther took it from my hands.

"Since your mother is gone," Tegan continued, "you have to take on her responsibilities." I looked over at Esther and watched as she peeled off the skin of the fruit.

"Like what?" he asked, finally looking up.

"Civil matters and such, just until we can choose the next *kiongozi*. That is unless you are willing to do it." The other women looked at him. Luca stared at his hands thoughtfully, then sighed.

"*Iwe hivyo [So be it]*. What do you need me to do?"

Esther nudged me and handed me my fruit back, which was now yellow and dripping juice. I smiled in thanks and took a bite.

"It's a mango. You don't eat the outside," Esther whispered, smirking.

"I think it's my new favorite fruit," I replied, wiping juice from my chin.

"Mine too," she said, bumping my shoulder with her own.

"What's a *kongozi*?" I asked a moment after Amla and Tegan took their conversation with Luca outside.

"Kiongozi," she corrected, "it's what we call the leader of the village. Usually the role goes to a female that the village voted for, but in the case of death or injury, her firstborn assumes the role until the next kiongozi is chosen."

"So the last one was Luca's mother?" I asked, taking a bite of my mango.

She nodded. "Kya was a great leader. She was young but wise beyond her years. We were so sad when she died." Esther shook her head. "I'm glad to see that Luca is doing better."

I swallowed the bit of fruit in my mouth thoughtfully. Thinking back, I felt bad for being mean to him for not coming to see me. He'd been dealing with Lonso and an entire village. "What was she like?"

"Oh Kya was beautiful. Luca looks just like her." Esther smiled ruefully. "She was the granddaughter of a previous kiongozi, but you couldn't tell. She was so down to earth that I remember her nursing injured baby dragons back to life after finding them in the mountains. Her mother wasn't too fond of that particular habit." She laughed.

"She really rescued baby dragons?" I asked, bewildered. From what Lonso told me, dragons were giant winged creatures that breathed fire. I couldn't imagine anyone going near them.

Esther nodded. "Those who live in Argo are the protectors of the dragons that live in our mountains. God gave them to us as a gift. It is our responsibility to take care of them. They are peaceful with us, but they absolutely loved Kya. She would spend afternoons in their dens." I raised my eyebrows in surprise. "They're quite fond of Luca too. I suppose they have the same spirit," she said with a wistful smile.

"If you don't mind, what was his father like?" I wiped my mouth and watched as her smile dropped.

"He was a terrible man, but I must not say anymore. Ask Luca if you like," she stated as she stood. She grabbed a cloth and handed it to me. I thanked her and wiped my mouth and hands. I understood that she felt it wasn't her place to tell me. I made a note to ask Luca later. I stood, dusting off my clothes. Esther handed me a bowl of water and a towel and a dress.

"I figured you'd want to change and wash up before dinner."

"Yes, thank you." I placed the bowl on the table next to me and took the clothes from her hands.

"Let me know when you're finished. I'll just be outside," she told me before leaving.

I stripped out of my clothes and bathed, grateful for the hot water she gave me. As I dried off, I couldn't help but think about what Esther told me. It made me feel even worse to think of how horrible I'd treated him when he finally came back to see me. I didn't know he was dealing with so much. I pulled on the dress and tied the straps around my neck. It was the same grassy material that everyone's clothes seemed to be made of. There was an intricate design of an eagle with broad wings in the middle of my chest. I pulled on my shoes and pulled my hair back into a bun. Padding to the door, I opened it and began to look around for Esther. All around were women gathered around a fire with large bowls in front of them. I turned at the sound of a whistle to see Esther waving me over. I jogged over to her and smiled at the women she was sitting next to.

"Ora, these are my friends, Rayna, Skye, and Alba," she told me as she pointed to each one.

"Hello." I smiled and waved as they all scooted over and patted the spot. I sat down, and they resumed their conversation. I watched as they cleaned and prepared vegetables for dinner.

"Hi, Ora." I looked up and saw Luca standing there, smiling as he looked me over.

"Hey," I replied, smiling back.

"Would you like to go for a walk with me?" Esther and her friends looked at me and giggled.

"Of course." He stretched out his hand and helped me up.

"Have fun you two," Esther called after us as we walked away.

Still holding my hand, he led me to the edge of the village. We walked down a path that led out and up the mountain. After a moment, he finally spoke, "So how do you like Argo so far?"

"I absolutely love it. It's so beautiful, and everyone is so nice," I expressed, smiling at my feet.

"I'm glad."

We continued down our path as the sun began to set behind us. I watched as the trees and leaves turned red in the glow of the setting sun. The light that peeked between the trees bounced off Luca's dark skin and made his orange eyes glow. He must have known I was staring because he turned and smiled at me. Blushing, I smiled and looked away. He chuckled and shook his head.

"Here we are," he told me as he helped me climb into the opening of the cave.

"Where are we?" I asked, looking around the cave. He grabbed my shoulders and turned me around. I gasped at the view. The sun shined between the mountaintops, casting a shadow over the village below. Tropical birds cawed in the distance as they flew into fruit and nut trees, trying to find their dinner.

"It's so beautiful. No wonder you love this place so much," I expressed, smiling.

"I really do." He turned and reached out to me. "Come, follow me." Holding my hand, he led me into the cave. As the light from outside dwindled, the darkness seemed to grow the deeper we walked. Suddenly there was a gust of wind that rushed from deep in the cave, blowing my hair behind me. My eyes widened as I slowed to a halt, my body drenched in fear.

"Luca?" My voice shook. All I could see was darkness. I swallowed the lump that rose in my throat and squeezed his hand. He didn't say anything, but as a low growl erupted in the cave, he let my hand go.

"Luca?" I whispered, trying to find him in the dark. "Luca!" After a moment of silence, I began to worry. As the fire emerged in the darkness, illuminating the cave, my eyes widened in horror. Just behind Luca was a huge scaly creature with big green eyes snarling at me.

"L-Luca," I stuttered, slowly backing up, "b-b-behind y-you."

He turned his head slowly and held out his arm to me. "Don't move." He slowly took a step toward the creature.

"Luca, no!" I hissed. What was he thinking? Ignoring me, he turned around to face the creature.

"*Shwari, shwari [calm]…*," he repeated as he kept walking while holding his hands out toward the creature. My heart raced as I watched him get closer and closer until his hand hovered over the creature's snout. I nearly peed my pants when he started petting it. After a moment, it stopped snarling at me and started to lean into his hand, purring. I shook in disbelief.

Luca leaned his head against its cheek as he continued petting it. "This is a dragon."

CHAPTER

3

"Don't make any sudden moves."

My eyes widened even more. "Don't make any sudden moves? It's a *freaking* dragon!" I pointed out. How could he expect me to be calm and collected with it being a mere five feet from me? I hesitantly looked away from the dragon who was still purring like a cat and leaning toward him.

"Luca, come on, let's—" I reached toward him, and the dragon growled, startling me.

"I told you not to make any sudden moves," he scolded as he tried to calm the dragon. "There, there, girl. She's just a friend." The creature's face left his hand and turned toward me. Her glowing green eyes focused on me as she took a cautious step toward me.

"Ora, just relax."

My eyes were locked with hers as my body shook in fear. Perspiration dripped into my eyes because I was too afraid she'd attack me if I tried to wipe it. She stopped just in front of me, sniffing my clothes. My breath grew heavy as I slowly looked up. Her big green eyes were focused and gleamed in the amber light. I started crying, too afraid to move an inch. Luca came around her side and patted her.

"She's a friend, Destiny, it's okay," he reassured her. She turned and looked at him briefly before returning her gaze to me. She came closer until her wide nostrils touched my cheeks. She let out a breath that blew my hair from my shoulders and put even more fear in me.

After a moment, she grunted and turned away. Sighing in relief, I was dumbfounded as I watched her lean into Luca and lick him.

"Destiny?" I asked, confused. He named her! How insane! I paused for a moment remembering what Esther said about him and his mother being loved by the dragons. My expression softened as I slumped to the floor. This was too much excitement for one day.

"*Umilele*," he told me in his native language. "I've known her since I was little. Her mother was my mother's favorite dragon," he told me smiling. "I wanted you to meet her."

"Well, thanks for the heads-up," I replied, flustered. I groaned as I lay on the cave floor trying to calm my racing heart. I threw an arm over my eyes and tried to relax. After a moment, the glow of the fire went out. I opened my eyes and jumped to see Destiny staring at me as she stood over me.

"Agh!"

"Come on," Luca said as he grabbed me by the arm and pulled me onto her neck where he was sitting. I clambered up her side and sat behind Luca. I swiftly grabbed him by the waist as she began walking, terrified of falling off.

"Where are we going?" I questioned as we exited the cave.

"We're going for a ride," he confessed as he grabbed a rope he'd put around her neck. I immediately moved to get down.

"Wait"—he laughed, reaching behind him to keep me in place—"it'll be fun."

"Why do you insist on trying to kill me?"

"Nothing bad will happen to you. I still plan to keep my promise," he reassured me. I let out a heavy sigh and moved to sit behind him again. "Just don't let me go," I snorted. *Trust me I didn't plan on it*, I thought to myself.

Destiny stretched her wings in the open space and let out a sound I can assume was a yawn.

"All right, girl, let's go. *Kuruka!*" She began to run the short distance off the cliff and jumped into the air. I screamed and held onto Luca for dear life. After a moment, I peeked through my closed eyes and made a noise.

"Ora, it's okay. Don't look down, just look around." I tried to calm my nerves as I felt his voice vibrating against my face and chest. I took a deep breath and opened my eyes. My cheek to his back, I looked at the beautiful scenery around me. The mountains were absolutely breathtaking. They were each created in their own unique way, showing different shades and hues of rock. Trees lined the bottom of the mountains forming a sort of barrier for them. Destiny soared through the sky, dipping and turning every which way. It took me awhile, but I eventually moved my head away from his back and began to enjoy myself. I regretted it almost immediately as she dived near a waterfall. She surprisingly landed gracefully on a rock, which made me feel a little better.

Luca slid down her side before he grabbed me by the hips and lifted me down.

"Where are we?"

"Someplace special." He smiled. He moved to the side so I could see the view better and my breath caught. A massive waterfall crashed down into a foaming river. The water gurgled as it glided over the rocks before calming as it joined the river. The bright sun peeked through trees as tall as the waterfall that must have housed thousands of birds, judging by the sweet songs they sang from their nests. I slowly looked around, taking in the gentle breeze that blew through the tall grass.

"It's beautiful." I gasped. If the rest of the world was as pretty as Argo, I couldn't wait to see it.

"Come on, follow me." He grabbed my hand and led me toward the waterfall. We walked along the rocks that outlined the river until we reached the side of the waterfall. Cold water sprayed onto my face as we stood beside it. My eyes widened as he walked closer and closer until he was completely inside of it. Still holding my hand, he pulled me through.

"What are you doing?" I asked, wiping water from my face.

"Look." With water still in my eyes, I squinted at my surroundings. We were in a sort of cave behind the waterfall. There were plants glowing with phosphorus all along the ground and drawings on the wall. Aside from the glow of the plants, it was kind of dark due to the clouds blocking out the light. Luca grabbed a blanket from his bag and laid it on the ground. He asked if I was hungry, and I nodded silently. He took out some food and laid it out. My eyebrows raised; he sure was prepared.

"I thought we could have a picnic," he explained as he unpacked the food.

"What's a picnic again?" He told me before, but I'd forgotten what he said.

"It's like a meal where you sit on the ground and eat outside," he explained. He dusted his hands off and sat beside me on the blanket. "My mom used to bring me here all the time. After my...*dad* left, she would come here and pray. Sometimes she wouldn't come back for at least a day," he remembered, his eyes sad.

"You don't speak about your dad a lot."

"I mean what's there to say? He was a horrible man who left my mother with two young kids. You'd think at such a vulnerable age, he'd be more considerate."

"If you don't mind me asking, what happened to your brother?"

"I never found out. I was at home one night, playing while my mom cooked dinner when someone came and got her. I heard mom crying, so I went outside to check on her. Baku was just lying there motionless in her arms. She never brought him up after the funeral," he confided in me.

"I'm sorry." He waved it off. "Where was your dad?" I inquired.

"He was there. He left soon after."

"Was that the last time you saw him?" I asked curiously.

"I saw him a few more times when I was younger. All I can remember about him is that I apparently look like him. I remember looking up at him at the funeral. The cold look in his eyes was disorienting," he explained. I could relate in a way. I couldn't even remember if I'd ever met my dad, let alone the way he looked. It's like with mother, just a faint memory.

"Where is he now?" I asked, pulling my knees to my chest.

"Who knows, probably off making someone else's life miserable." He opened a package and offered it to me. I grabbed a sandwich and took a bite. "I'd like to change the subject, though." I nodded as I chewed.

"Do you have any siblings?" he asked, crossing his legs as he grabbed a handful of grapes.

"No, well, I don't know. All I can remember are my mom's face and the flowers in the forest we were in when we got separated. It never occurred to me that I may have siblings," I told him honestly. What if I did have someone out there who looked like me? Were they locked up too?

He looked at me with sympathy. Every day I wondered if I'd ever see her again. I wondered if she was even alive. Luca placed his hand on mine, and I opened my eyes.

"It'll be okay," he promised. I took a deep breath and nodded. We continued to eat in silence, stuck in our individual thoughts. My mind wandered as I nibbled on some cheese. The setting sun cast rainbows of colors through the cascading water and into the cave. I watched the light dance on the water as I pulled my hair into a bun.

"You know, I really like your hair," Luca complimented. I smiled and looked away. Wrapping the last lock around my bun, I dusted off my hands and popped the last piece of fruit into my mouth. Luca began to put away the leftovers, then stood, dusting his hands on his pants. He held out a hand, helping me up. I took it gratefully, but once I stood, he didn't let it go.

"Walk with me." I nodded and closed my eyes as we walked back through the waterfall. We climbed down the sides of the bank and started down a trail. I loved how there were so many flowers in Argo. Everywhere you roamed, there were flowers in all shapes and colors. We walked slowly so I could admire each one, but one especially caught my attention.

"What kind of flower is this?" I asked, stooping down beside it.

"It's a flame vine." He squatted next to me. "It's Argo's main flower." I touched the delicate petals. It was an orange flower shaped like a trumpet, but unlike other flowers, there were a lot of them surrounding the single one.

"Is this all one plant?"

He nodded. "It's a vine, so all of these flowers came from the same plant."

"Wow."

It was amazing to think it started as a single seed. Now the plant covered a large area along the path. Luca plucked off one of the flowers and put it in my bun. Our eyes met and held each other for a moment. His beautiful eyes matched the flowers behind him, both like flames. He reached up and caressed my cheek, and I closed my eyes as I leaned into it. After a moment, he moved his hand with a small smile.

Our walk was pretty silent after that. Neither of us talked about what just happened but rather focused on things we saw along the path.

"Sooo...," I said, trying to make this less awkward, "you must be happy to be back?"

"I am." He nodded as he dragged a stick he found along the dirt.

"Do your friends know you're here?"

He snorted, "Friends?"

"Yeah, friends. You know, the people you hang out with, have things in common with?" I egged on.

"I don't have any friends here. I just have you." He looked up at me.

"Wow, you must be a terrible person then," I joked. He chuckled and continued walking. We eventually reached the end of the trail and decided it was time to head back. The sun had now set, and the only light came from the moon and the big gray clouds in the night sky. He whistled, and Destiny came flying over. We mounted her and flew to the edge of the village. Presumably because if she landed any closer, she would probably knock a house or something down. After getting down, Luca ran his hand across her neck and patted her a few times. She made a low noise before turning and flying away. We watched her as she disappeared into the clouds.

"Hello, you two." Esther smiled. She stood there with a basket in her hands and her hair wrapped up. Her smile said she was up to something.

"Hi," we said in unison.

"I took the liberty of feeding your little friend here," she told me as she handed me Peto.

"Thank you." I smiled. I had completely forgotten to feed him before I left. He slithered along my cheek, and I knew that was his way of saying it was okay.

"So"—Esther clasped her hands together with a smirk—"how was your date?"

I looked up at Luca who groaned and rolled his eyes. She held up her hands and chuckled as Luca grabbed my hand and led me to the house. We walked over to the one I was in before, and he stopped at the door.

"Get some sleep, Ora. There's a lot to do tomorrow." I nodded silently, and he turned to walk away.

"Wait! Where are you going?" I asked nervously.

"To my house."

"You're not staying with me?" I asked in a panic. He shook his head, and my face fell. He bent down and gave me a kiss on the cheek.

"You'll be fine. Plus, I'll be over first thing in the morning."

"Don't worry, we'll have a sleepover." Esther winked at me before going inside. I bit my lip and stared at him for a moment.

"You'll be fine, promise," he reassured me. I nodded and wished him good night before walking inside. The open space from earlier was now set out with beds. Esther came over and handed me some clothes.

"To sleep in," she told me. I placed Peto on a ledge by the dresser where he could sleep comfortably. I stripped down and changed, folding my clothes into a neat pile for tomorrow. I straightened out the nightgown and walked over to the bowl of water to splash some on my face. Esther offered me a towel, and I accepted.

"So where did you lovebirds go?"

"He took me to this cave and to a waterfall," I replied, patting my face dry.

She nodded knowingly. "Ah his favorite places, how nice. Did you meet Umilele?"

"Yes. After a heart-attack-inducing introduction, we did meet." Esther's laugh made me think this wasn't the first time he failed to mention his dragon to someone.

"Luca is wise. They're endangered creatures. He will only introduce her to those he trusts," she explained. I was deeply touched hearing that. "You like him?"

"Like who?"

"Luca." My brow furrowed. Of course, I liked him; he was my friend. Though I had a feeling that's not what she meant. "Do you want to be with him?" She prodded.

"I do like him. He's my friend, so of course. I don't think he likes me the way you mean, though."

She tilted her head and examined me. "Men like Luca are not the type to pressure a woman. I think he does, but he just wants to get to know you more first."

I shrugged. "Maybe."

She sucked her teeth before walking over to blow out the candle that illuminated the room. We said good night, and she shuffled to her bed and lay down. It only took her a moment to fall asleep and begin snoring loudly. I turned to lay on my back and stared at the ceiling. I contemplated what Esther said. I didn't think Luca liked me just because he was nice to me. The more I thought, the more I began to think about him—his tall stature, his beautiful luminescent eyes that seemed to almost glow in the sunset, the way his face lit up when he smiled... I shook my head. I chalked my thoughts up to Esther teasing me and went to sleep.

*****

I woke up early the next morning to the light peeking through the window. I yawned and turned to see Esther's bed made and empty. I stood and stretched as I looked around. I walked over to the table, which had a bowl of fruit and a basket of bread. There was something I assumed was eggs in a container beside them. Next to the bread was a note from Esther letting me know this was my food and she had gone to work. I chewed on my bread, watching Peto slither down the ledge he was sitting on and onto my arm.

"Good morning, Peto." He ran his face against my cheek before draping himself around my neck.

I quickly finished eating, then changed into my clothes from the day before. I made sure Peto was securely on my neck before opening the front door. I stepped into the fresh morning air and took a deep breath. It smelled of campfire and morning dew. There weren't many people around aside from those walking to and fro. Their low chatter was masked by the sound of tropical birds calling in the trees above. I looked around for any sign of Luca but had no luck. Unsure of his whereabouts, I decided to explore Argo. I started down a dirt path that crinkled under my sandals. Further up the path was a woman hanging clothes up on a line. I headed toward her.

"Hello," I greeted. She looked up from her basket and smiled.

"Why, hello there. How are you this morning?"

"I'm good, how are you?" I asked, happy I had someone to talk to.

"I'm good, I'm good," she repeated as she held her basket on her hip as she used her hand to block the sun out of her eyes. "What can I help you with?"

"I was wondering if you needed any help?"

Her smile grew bigger. "I'd love that, thank you."

She asked me to hold her basket while she pinned the clothes up, explaining how much her back hurts from the constant bending. I happily held it for her as she told me about herself. She was in her early forties and had three children. She talked about how busy they kept her, and despite being a handful, they were the joy of her life. She was married to a man on the council, so she stayed at home and took care of the kids and house.

"I don't know, sometimes I feel like a raggedy old lady," she expressed as I helped her fold laundry.

"You aren't old at all! You're still young and beautiful. I know your husband is happy he found you," I complimented. She was beautiful. She had auburn hair and freckles that sprinkled across her honey skin. Her orange eyes were framed by thick eyelashes that dusted her cheeks. She was shorter than me but had ample curves that were only partially hidden by her modest wrap skirt and shirt.

"Thank you," she replied, blushing. Her eyes widened as she slapped her hands over her mouth. "I'm so sorry, I'm so rude. I didn't even ask you your name!"

I laughed. "I'm Ora."

"Adara, nice to meet you. So what brings you to Argo?"

"I'm here with a friend. I didn't have a place to go, so he brought me here." She nodded as if she understood.

"Who's your friend?" she replied. I was grateful she didn't press for more information that I wasn't sure I wanted to give up.

"Luca."

"Ah that makes sense. He is such a sweet boy. Shame how he lost his mother." I nodded, remembering his expression when he talked about her. She looked at me quizzically. "Not to alarm you, but there's a snake on you."

I'd completely forgotten about Peto. He was hiding in my pocket and now was slithering up my arm. "I know, he's mine. This is Peto."

"Hi, Peto," she greeted, running a finger across his white scales.

"Well, that's the last of that," she announced as she folded the last piece of clothing. "I'll put these away and make us a snack." She smiled, leading us into the house. I looked around the room as I waited. It was similar to Esther's but with some personal touches. There were two large sofas facing each other only separated by a nicely decorated coffee table that held a bowl of sand and some candles. Her walls were tan and the floor concrete. A thick shaggy rug kept my feet warm as I sat on the couch. It was an elaborate pattern of different colors. A unique light fixture dangled from the ceiling, letting in light along with the many windows in the room. She had family photos and children's art scattered along the walls as if they were gallery pieces. My eyes lingered on a colorful drawing of a purple dragon that breathed blue fire. It was surrounded by trees and flowers that peeked from under its big legs. The drawing was clearly drawn by a young child, but it made me wonder if there are more dragons living in Argo. As I walked along the walls, examining each photo, I noticed that all of the kid drawings were of dragons.

"Adara?" I called.

"Yes?" she yelled from the back.

"How many dragons live in Argo?"

"Oh girl, more than we can count. They're kind of sacred around here. That's why the council is so adamant about keeping them safe," she replied, bustling in the other room.

I looked down at the pictures again, curious about whether these drawings were accurate on their appearance. After a moment or two, Adara came in with a tray of food that she placed on the coffee table before sitting across from me. She handed me a bowl and settled into her seat with her own.

"Tell me about yourself, Ora."

"Well, there isn't much to tell really. I was separated from my mother at a very young age, and it wasn't until recently that I met Luca and he brought me here."

"How did you guys get separated?" she asked with a sad expression on her face.

"I can only remember bits and pieces, and from what I can remember, someone was chasing us, and they took her away and put me in a uh…facility." I didn't dare say prison. It was bad enough I had to live there my whole life, but just the thought of telling everyone I met made me cringe.

"That's so sad. I'm so sorry." She frowned. "I lost my dad in the war when I was just a kid. It's something you'll always carry with you." She stuck a fork in a berry and ate it.

"The war?" I asked, curious.

She nodded. "Some years ago, there was a war that broke out. Essentially it was over the dragons. There were a group of people who wanted to use the dragon's abilities to colonize other villages and 'make us stronger,'" she said using air quotations, "but people like my dad were against it. They believed that Argonians were here to protect them, not to abuse them. So the opposing group decided to ignore the wishes of the majority and snuck up to the mountain and tried to wrestle down a dragon so they could tame it. Needless to say, it didn't go well. The poor thing luckily got away, but the leaders supposedly got this nasty scar on his face and neck from the struggle."

"Once the council got wind of it, they were furious. The leader continued to defy them and argue until they eventually broke out into a fight. It lasted a few months, but a lot of people died. Once it ended, they banished those that were left of the group."

"Wow," I said after a moment, "I'm sorry about your dad."

"Thanks. It's okay though because he died fighting for what he believed was right. He always said that was the only way to live."

We sat there silently thinking about our lost parents. After a beat, we ate and finished our food, and I walked into the kitchen to help her clean up.

"I enjoyed your company today, Ora," she said, throwing a dish towel onto the counter.

"I enjoyed you too. I've never had any girl friends, so I'm kind of new to all of this."

"Well, now you do." She smiled and touched my shoulder. We said our goodbyes, and I left her house. It appeared to be around noon, judging by the position of the sun. I walked around aimlessly as I tried to find Luca.

"Ora!" Someone called behind me. I turned to see Luca jogging up to me.

"Where have you been? I've been looking for you all morning," he asked, visibly upset.

"I'm sorry."

He sighed. "It's okay, I'm just glad you're okay. I was getting worried. Are you hungry?"

I shook my head. "No, I ate with Adara."

"Adara?"

"That's where I was. I was helping a woman named Adara with some housework." I motioned toward her house down the road.

"Okay, but please try not to wander off next time. Try not to go into anyone else's house that you don't know," he added. I nodded, and he grabbed me by the hand.

"Come on, I want you to come with me to this meeting."

"What is the meeting for?"

"The elders wanted me to come sit in on their meeting. They want me to be more aware of what's going on, I guess."

"I may just be imagining it, but you don't sound too enthused about this."

"That's because I'm not."

We walked into a building and saw a group of people sitting in a circle, one of which was Esther. She waved and motioned over, but Luca continued to hold my hand, so I sat beside him. *Maybe he just needed some encouragement,* I thought.

"Now that everyone is here, we can begin." The man who spoke was up in age and had a long black beard and thick locks like mine. His old eyes were shadowed by a pair of round glasses, which he adjusted every so often. His voice was deep and gruff as he spoke.

"First thing is first. Welcome, Luca, we appreciate you coming. However"—he looked over at me, his glasses low on his nose—"it is not appropriate for your friend to be joining us."

"She stays," he declared, squeezing my hand.

"What we plan to discuss is information that should only be privy to the elders and you," he shot back.

I turned to Luca. "I can go if it's a problem—"

"No," he cut me off, "I need you here." He turned back to face the man. "She stays," he told him as if daring him to protest again. The old man opened his mouth to speak but was interjected by Esther.

"Elijah, I have met Ora, and she is a lovely young lady. Our information is safe with her. Besides, I'm sure Luca wants someone familiar with him to make him more comfortable being here," the old man snorted and looked away.

"Young lady," I turned to face a woman that looked similar to Elijah, "this information must not be repeated."

"I won't," I promised. She nodded, seeming satisfied with my devotion to secrecy and began the meeting.

"Now"—she clasped her hands together—"let's start with a word of prayer."

The meeting went on for quite some time as they discussed everything from food production to issues with neighboring villages.

"Luca, have you come to a decision yet?" The woman who looked like Elijah turned out to be his twin sister Eva. Her gaze was now fixated on Luca.

"Not yet," he replied.

"Please come up with a decision soon," the woman told him, "we need your answer right away."

"I'll try." He looked away, glancing at me.

"Thank you all for coming. We have much to deliberate." She glanced at Luca. "We shall meet again in a few days."

Everyone stood and waited for Eva and Elijah to leave, then began to talk amongst themselves. Luca sat beside me with his face in his hands.

"Are you okay?"

He shook his head and remained silent. I managed to get him to stand and grabbed his hand. I walked us back to Esther's house. I figured he needed somewhere private to sort out his feelings. I sat across from him on the floor and waited until he was ready to speak.

"I can't do this, Ora." I waited for him to finish. "I can't lead these people. I don't know what I'm doing."

"Why not tell them that then?" I suggested.

He shook his head. "They've had this long tradition for generations. Someone in my family has to be in charge."

"Then we find someone else to do it."

"The only other person is Esther." He looked up at me. "But she is old. I cannot ask her to do that for me."

We both sighed as we realized what he said was true. Esther was old, and to ask her to spend the rest of her days taking care of the people seemed a bit selfish. And if something were to happen to her, they would just look to Luca again.

I patted his hand. "It will be all right. Personally I believe you can do it. You are a natural-born leader," I assured him. He placed his hand on mine and smiled. Our eyes met, and we gazed at each other for a moment, but then he turned and looked away. His hands were now knitted across his knees as he sat, looking around. I continued to look at him wondering how it felt to have people need you so badly, to want to live in a way that you were not destined to live. I could only imagine what he must be going through.

My stomach growled loudly, interrupting my thoughts. The sun was now setting, and I was starting to get hungry.

"Someone's hungry." He chuckled.

"I really am. All I had today was breakfast," I replied, holding my stomach. The hunger was so immense that my stomach felt like it was on fire.

"Come on, I'll make you something." He stood and helped me up.

"You cook?" He laughed.

"Yes, I cook. Let's go to my house so I can get started."

"Your house?" I realized I'd never asked about simple things like where he lived and if he knew how to cook.

"Yes, the place I live." He laughed. "What, did you think I was homeless or something?"

"I mean not exactly…" he continued laughing at me as he walked out the door. I followed him down the trail to the edge of town where a fairly large house was built.

"This is the chief's house. It's been in my family since the first chief came to power," he explained. The house had a front porch with large columns shooting up toward the sky. An artisan wood door was framed with baskets of flowers on the porch. Just beside the building to the right was a field of those flowers I saw in the woods. "Flame vine," he said.

"How come there are so many different houses here?" I asked. I'd seen three different styles today alone.

"Well, the chief's house is always unique. Others build their homes how they want. Esther chose the original house design from our ancestors from centuries ago. She said it preserves the history."

He unlocked the door, and I walked into a large open-concept area. To my left was the living room with its large furnishings and beautiful paintings on the walls. A shag rug anchored the entire area's aesthetic. To my right was the dining area, which was centered with a long wooden table that held well over twelve people. The fabric on the puffy cushions attached to the chairs glistened against the light from the chandelier. Pictures of what I assumed to be family members created a collage against the backwall. Straight ahead was a massive kitchen complete with wall-to-wall counters and an island. Just above the sink was an arch that had little baskets assembled for dishrags and such. He walked straight into the kitchen heading toward the fridge. I followed behind him, eager to watch what he planned on making. I plopped down into a barstool and rested my face in my hands. I watched as he bustled around the kitchen, grabbing items from different cabinets and banging the pots as he retrieved them from their rightful places. It didn't take long before a wonderful smell began to waft its way toward my nose. The food sizzles in the pan as he throws something over it and turns the heat off. He plated the food and set it down in front of me complete with lemonade and silverware. He sat beside me with his and said a quick prayer before putting a spoonful in my mouth. I don't know what it was, but it was amazing.

"It's jollof rice with chicken." I took my spoon from him and shoved some more in my mouth.

"This is so good." I moaned as I continued eating.

"Well, I'm glad you like it." He smiled before diving into his own plate. He handed me some bread, coco bread he said it was, and the combination got only more heavenly. I sopped up the last of my rice with bread and leaned back, completely content.

"You can be my new personal chef now," I expressed, rubbing my now full tummy. He chuckled and put our dishes in the sink. After helping him clean up, he led me to the living room and pulled a box down from the shelf by the table. He opened the box and pulled out a stack of old photographs. He went through each one, pointing out relatives and telling me funny stories. He stopped on a photo that I assumed was his mother. He handed me the picture, and I gasped. Her beauty was almost angelic, and she had the sweetest smile. Luca was maybe a teenager standing between her and Lonso on the beach, wearing the biggest smile.

"You must really miss them. I sure miss Lonso," I said, staring at Lonso's face. I still couldn't believe he was gone. He nodded slowly before putting the picture back in the box. He looked up at the clock and back at me.

"Movie?"

"Yes." I smiled. He popped in a movie, then grabbed a blanket for us.

*****

I woke up in a comfortable bed wrapped in warm sheets. I wiggled my toes, wondering where my shoes were. Yawning, I sat up and stretched. I looked around, wondering where I was. Memories flooded back to me, and I grabbed a blanket from the bed and wrapped it around me. I walked out of the room and into the hallway toward the kitchen, pouring myself some water. I set my glass down and walked over to the couch where Luca was sleeping. His head rested on a pillow, and a blanket draped over his large frame. I squatted in front of him and tapped his shoulder. He slowly opened his orange eyes and smiled before closing them again.

"Good morning, Ora."

"Good morning. Hey how did I get in the bed?"

"You fell asleep during the movie, so I carried you there. I figured it'd be more comfortable than this couch," he replied as he stretched, and his back cracked. "Are you hungry?" He finally opened his eyes again. I nodded, and he chuckled.

"Give me a minute."

I sat on the couch and rewrapped myself in my blanket cocoon. Luca began humming as he made breakfast. The sounds must have made me fall asleep because I woke up to him tapping me and holding a plate. I yawned and grabbed it thankfully before scarfing it down.

"So what's the plan for today?" I asked, wiping my mouth.

"I thought I'd show you more of our culture," he told me.

"Oh that sounds great. What are we doing first?"

"First, you are going to brush your teeth." He laughed as he fanned his nose. I punched him in the arm and rolled my eyes.

After he got dressed, we made a pit stop at Esther's house so I could wash up and change. I put back on the outfit I arrived in, my sweater and jeans, then ran outside to meet Luca. First thing he showed me was the village. Although I'd been there for a while now, he still felt it necessary to go over it. He explained that the houses were built in a pattern.

"Each house was built to hold the family of each occupation. So my house is the family chief house, then next to mine are the council members, then the medic, teacher, and so on before you get to family homes for everyone else."

"What does everyone else do?"

"Well, in general, everyone helps with growing food and harvesting it, making baskets and other tools, but some have their specialties that they do to make money. Like specialty fruits or flowers they'll grow in their backyard or jewelry. Some even make furniture," he explained.

He guided me through the rest of the village showing me the fields of food they grew or the grove of fruit and nut trees. He even weaved me a basket, which I had to admit was very impressive how quickly he made it. It was a wonderful day filled with fun and wonder. Children giggled as they played outside in the sun. It was a beautiful day that now was transitioning into a vibrant sunset. At the end of our tour, he led me to a spring of water that they got all of their drinking water from. We sat beside it and watched the sun go down as my head rested on his shoulder.

*****

Every morning, Luca picked me up and walked me to his house for breakfast. I could tell he was up to something by the huge grin he'd been wearing since he said good morning.

"I am going to teach you how to cook," he told me. I side-eyed him and shook my head vigorously. I knew it.

"Uh, I don't think that will be necessary. Besides, I enjoy having you cook for me," I told him, smiling sweetly. I dug my heels into the ground as he pushed me toward the kitchen.

"As much as I enjoy cooking for you, and I do, it is a skill you need to learn." He stood me in front of the stove and placed a pan on top of the burner.

"When your house burns down, do not blame me," I warned him.

"I won't let it. We're just making eggs, easiest thing in the world."

He pulled milk, butter, eggs, and seasoning salt out of their respective places and placed them on the counter. He placed a bowl directly in front of me and handed me an egg.

"Just tap it on the counter and break it in the bowl," he instructed, demonstrating. He handed me an egg, and I tapped it on the counter. It didn't crack, so I hit it a bit harder. It broke, and the insides dripped all over the counter. I held up my slimy hand and looked at Luca.

"It's okay, try again." He laughed.

"I don't want to," I pouted.

"Come on, I'll help you." He put his hand over mine and gently cracked the egg. We used our fingers to pull the shell apart over the bowl, dropping the insides in the bowl. The next one, I cracked by myself. It was good until I had to pick some of the shell out of the bowl.

"Good, now a splash of milk, and now we whisk." He handed me a wooden spoon. I mixed slowly until it was smooth. He turned on the stove and put a pad of butter into the sizzling pan. He poured the eggs into the pan and sprinkled it with seasoning salt. I stirred until he said they were done, and voila, eggs!

"Ah! I did it!" I squealed with glee.

"See? Easy." I plated our eggs and sat beside him on a stool. *Mmm*, cooking might not be so bad after all.

After breakfast, Luca had a big meeting to attend. The elders gave him until today to make a decision about becoming the kiongozi. We now stood outside the door, waiting a moment to go in.

"You are the definition of a kiongozi, no one is more fit for this job than you," I encouraged. He smiled when I pronounced kiongozi correctly. I'd learned a few words from Esther when I wasn't hanging out with Luca.

"You think so?"

"I know so." I shook his shoulders, making him laugh. "Now get in there and dominate."

He took a deep breath and went inside. I wasn't allowed in the meetings after the first one. Esther assured me she's there if he needed her. I made my way down the path and headed toward Adara's house.

I walked up her path and knocked on the door. He opened the door breathless, his hair wild on top of her head.

"Hey girl."

"Hey, I'm not waking you up, am I?" I asked, looking at her disheveled appearance.

"Ha! I wish! No, the kids are home from school today. It's been a bit crazy." She stepped aside, letting me in. She wasn't joking when she said things were crazy. Toys were on every surface of the floor, along with various articles of clothing and crumbs. I could hear kids screaming and crying in the back, making her run to their aid. I kneeled down and started picking up toys and putting them in bins that sat against the wall. Once all of the toys were picked up, I folded the clothes, sat them on the couch, and swept the floor. Turns out the little chores Lonso made me do as a kid were useful after all.

She came back in with a toddler on her hip and the other two in tow behind her.

"You really are an angel," she said, looking at the living room that was now clean. I laughed and kneeled in front of her kids who hid behind her skirt.

"Hi, I'm Ora," I said to them. Although they were boys of varying ages, they all looked exactly like Adara with their freckles and auburn hair. The younger one had big eyes, which he batted at me as he sucked on his thumb. The older one came from around her and stuck his hand out.

"*Jambo*!" he yelled. I laughed, standing up, wiggling the toddler's toes.

"They are so cute." The two boys ran to the kitchen and rummaged through the cabinets.

"Thank you, they're a mischievous bunch, but they are cute. Hard to stay mad at them." She ruffled the baby's hair, and he smiled, revealing dimples. "This little guy is Amare, he's one, the bold one is Enoch who is six, and the shy one is Ode, he's three."

They were all beautiful. It made me a bit sad because I was no older than Enoch when I was taken from my mother.

"Do you need help with anything?" I asked, dragging myself from my thoughts.

"Uhm, no but we were just going for a walk if you'd like to join us." She placed the younger kids in a stroller and packed a small bag full of snacks and water. She pulled the bag onto her back, and we headed outside.

The walk was relaxing. The kids seemed to enjoy it too because they fell asleep halfway through it. Enoch ran a bit ahead of us, playing in the flowers. He'd occasionally backtrack to give us a flower he picked up. I smiled as I held my small bouquet of wildflowers. Enoch smiled up at me, grabbing my hand. He was a little flirt for sure.

We walked back to the house as it started to sprinkle. Enoch weighed heavy in my arms as he slept on my shoulder. Once inside, I laid him gently on his bed, pulling the cover over him, and tiptoed back to the front door. Adara met me on the other side. She held her hands in her armpits as she ducked under the awning that shielded her from the rain.

"I'm sorry we couldn't do more," she apologized.

"No, it's okay really. I had fun." She smiled, reached over, and squeezed my hand. We said our goodbyes, and I ran through the rain back to Esther's house. The sky was dark, and the thunder rumbled as I splashed through the puddles. Once inside, I took off my shoes and changed out of my wet clothes. I was ringing out my hair into a bucket when Esther and Luca walked in.

"*Neno langu* [My word]," Esther muttered under her breath. She shook the rain from her clothes and untied her sandals. Luca stood beside her, snickering as he dripped onto her carpet. He looked up and smiled as he noticed me. His smile sparkled like the water droplets in his hair.

"You got caught in it too, huh?" He took off his boots, placing them beside mine.

"Sadly." I squeezed the last section of locks into the bucket. Despite being rung dry, they still felt heavy, so I decided to leave them hanging loose around my shoulders. Esther gave me a kiss on the cheek before making her way into the kitchen. Mere moments passed before I heard the familiar sounds of cooking.

Luca emptied my bucket outside before coming to sit across from me.

"So how did it go?" I inquired.

"I decided to accept the role of kiongozi."

"Ah! I'm so happy for you! You'll make an amazing kiongozi. Congratulations."

"I wanted to tell you thank you." He looked at me, his smile warming me up.

"For the speech?" I joked.

"That too"—he laughed—"but for believing in me, even when I was questioning my own abilities," he thanked me, still smiling.

"Of course. I've always got your back." I winked.

"So what were you up to while I was gone?"

I recounted my brief day with Adara and her children. I even mentioned how Enoch flirted with me.

"And how old is this kid?" he asked with a lowered brow.

"He's six going on twenty-six," I busted out laughing. Luca shook his head as he helped me up from the floor. Esther was done with dinner and had called us to eat. To say it smelled heavenly was a complete understatement.

After dinner I sat between Esther's legs as she washed, cleaned, and retwisted my locks. It was an extremely long process to say the least. She began by washing my scalp, an experience that has definitely made it to my top ten favorite things. Afterward she soaked my hair in a concoction that took out what I assume to be years of buildup from inside of my locks. Once she rinsed them and rung them dry, they were light as a feather. I stroked one as she retwisted the rest of my hair.

"Luca, how do you say you're a miracle worker in Swahili?" I asked with wide eyes.

"Wewe ni mfanyikazi wa miujiza." He snickered.

"Wewe ni mfyanikazi wa mujzia," I attempted.

"Miujiza," Luca corrected.

"Miujiza," I repeated.

"Ah, very good. And it is nothing really, just a simple mixture I use on my own hair. And there, all done," she replied, dropping the last lock into place.

"Thank you."

"You are so welcome."

They both laughed at me as I swung them from side to side. Light as a feather.

*****

"Alora, stay here," my mom instructed as she pushed me away from the door.

"But mo—" I protested.

"Stay here!" She shoved me into the closet and locked the door behind her. I whimpered in the darkness, too afraid of the shadows that danced behind me.

"You must be quiet," she scolded.

I pressed my tiny hands over my mouth as tears rolled down my cheeks.

*****

I blinked the tears away as I adjusted my eyes to the light. I sat up and rubbed my face, trying to hide my tears. There was a soft hum of conversation coming from the kitchen where Luca and Esther were talking. It was early, the sun just starting to rise. I quietly stood and walked into the bathroom. I hadn't had a nightmare since I left my cell. It seemed that with each new dream, another piece of my past was revealed. My last moments with my mother. I splashed some cold water on my face and tried to think about other things. Like the fact that the sun was not only out but was shining brightly through the windows. Glad that I'd bathed the night before, I pulled on my clothes and walked outside. I sighed, content in the warm breeze and sunshine. I made my way down a path and lay in the first large space of grass I saw. Ever since I'd left my cell, I have loved grass. I wiggled in it getting comfortable as I stared up at the clouds, making out shapes. I was creating a story based on my cloud creatures when Adara plopped down in the grass beside me.

"That one looks like a dancing lady," she said, pointing.

"Are you referring to my trumpeting angel?" I argued, "Because if you are, I will tell you he is well on his way to music school. He has played that trumpet his entire life, ever since he was given it by his great-grandfather. For you to call him a dancing lady is not only an insult to him but his talent as well."

She turned her head and busted out laughing. "Will he make the audition?"

"It's unclear. The other angels think he is terrible, but he's determined to be the best. You know, for Grandpappy."

"For Grandpappy!" she yelled, sending us into a fit of laughter.

CHAPTER

An ear-piercing roar bellowed through the village. We paused and looked around in the darkness trying to find out where it came from. The night was quiet except for chirping crickets and the buzz of insects flying. We held our breath and waited. Growls escaped through the trees, sending tremors down my spine. I looked over at Luca, who was focused on a shadow in the distance. Suddenly a woman's scream released into the air as a house was set on fire. We raced over to the house. Luca was trying to save the woman as I threw pails of water at the house. Luca successfully rescued a woman and her two children who were crying uncontrollably. I managed to get the fire out quickly before it spread, but my heart sank after I turned to tell Luca. Every house was on fire. People were screaming and crying as they watched their homes burn to ash. Luca was standing perfectly still, and I followed his eyes and saw the culprits. A group of men riding a beast of some kind that spewed fire on house after house. Luca charged toward them before I could stop him. Several men dissipated from the man in the center and began to terrorize people. Luca's eyes were locked on the man as he yelled running faster and faster. Screams became louder as I watched the men slaughter people before my very eyes. Everyone was in chaos running and trying to hide only to remember that their houses were on fire. Luca had disappeared from sight in the dark, and I panicked. The sky was bright red from the fire as an immense heat began to radiate around me.

"Run into the woods. Go hide," I told the woman and her children. She nodded and ran as fast as she could with her babies. I waited until she was safely in the brush to move. I had to find Luca. I ran through the village as fast as I could until I heard a voice I recognized.

"How *dare* you come here and attack us!" Esther scolded a man on the creature. I ran to her side and pulled her behind me. The man was tall with a mask that concealed his face. His uniform was the color of dark blood and black. Up close, the creature he rode was even more terrifying. It was black with yellow spots with a round head that held sharp teeth. Its long tail swayed in agitation as he stood there. The man said nothing; he just stared, breathing deeply. I froze.

Esther pushed me back behind her and went in on him.

"How could you do this?" she asked, sounding almost upset, as if she were about to cry. The creature growled at her, but he pulled the reins and dipped his head before running off. She watched him run right out of the village. I wanted to ask her what was going on but remembered I needed to find Luca.

"I can't find Luca."

"I'll help you find him."

We began looking around for him, crying the longer it took. Bodies were strewn on the ground, some yelling in pain and others not at all.

"Look." Esther pointed up ahead at a tousle that involved fire.

"Luca!" I screamed as I started to run forward before Esther grabbed me and covered my mouth.

"Let me go. I have to help him!" I yelled.

"Help with what? You will only be a distraction and get in the way. He will be fine," she assured me.

"But how do you know?"

She patted my shoulder. "I just do. Trust me."

She led us closer to them but away enough so that we weren't seen. Luca was punching the creature repeatedly until the man fell off. The creature, clearly injured, whimpered before running away, leaving the man. Luca was fuming, and so were his hands. They glowed with fire, but he didn't seem bothered, as if it didn't burn. I shook my head. This didn't make sense. Why were his hands on fire?

He punched the air twice as fireballs shot from his hands and at the man who fell backward at the impact. After getting up, he shot a few fire shots at Luca who easily dodged them before shooting a ray of fire at the man. He coughed and wheezed as he tried to not inhale the smoke coming from his singed uniform.

"Call them off," Luca barked.

"Never," the man said. Luca formed an open flame in his open hand.

"Call them off." He sneered between clenched teeth. The man coughed again before he blew something around his neck. Suddenly a creature ran up behind Luca and smacked him a few feet with his tail. His rider quickly led him over to the leader and picked him up. The rest followed in pursuit as they disappeared into the forest.

I ran over to Luca with tears welling in my eyes.

"Luca! Luca! Please tell me you're okay!" I cried, turning him over onto his back. He groaned in pain, and I hugged him. I checked him over, and it didn't seem as if he was bleeding anywhere. I sighed in relief and hugged him again.

"Ora? Are you okay?" he mumbled before coughing hard. He sat up trying to catch his breath.

"You left me." I cried, the tears I'd been holding in finally falling.

"I'm sorry. I'm just glad you're okay."

"That was a foolish thing to do, leaving her to fight someone," Esther told him.

"I was just doing my job as chief." I helped him stand up. "I figured if I stopped the guy in charge, they all would leave," he told her honestly.

"Yes, they'd leave, and she could have been dead." Clutching his side, he searched my eyes for a moment, her words ringing in his ears.

"I'm so sorry for leaving you, Ora. You are okay, aren't you?"

I nodded. "But a lot of people aren't," I told him, motioning toward the survivors who were now checking on those who were injured or worse.

Luca blew his shell on his neck, and people gathered. Despite his injuries, he divided up the survivors into groups. One group was tasked with assisting the medic, who we were all grateful had survived, in bringing him all of the wounded. Another group wrote down all those who had died and made a note of those who were missing. The third group was tasked with putting out the fires. I ran back to the house and went to the entrance of the forest trying to find the woman and her children. I walked a little deeper in and found her and a group of people and children. I told them it was safe and they were gone but to keep the children there so we could get everything settled.

"I don't think they should see this." She nodded and sent a group of adults to help. Once they had all of the dead in a specific spot, they all came out.

Bodies were lined up with blankets draped over their lifeless bodies. People cried as they went to identify their loved ones. My heart welled at the sight of so many people. I held the woman and her children as they cried over a dead husband/father.

"Luca!" a man called from the back of the village.

Luca jogged over to him. After a moment of talking, they ran up the hill. After what seemed like a long time, they returned. Luca was once again visibly furious.

"What's wrong?" He shook his head, too angry to speak. I grabbed his face in my hands. "Take a deep breath. You cannot lead them without a cool head, and they need you now more than ever." He nodded and tried to breathe. He eventually calmed down.

"Thanks." He called everyone once more, and they all sat down in front of him. "I don't know who exactly attacked us, but I promise you I will find out who did," he assured the crowd, looking around. "It has come to my attention that the attack was just a distraction. While some were here, many of them were in the mountains." People began to whisper amongst themselves, but Luca raised his hand to stop them.

"They were trying to take the dragons. Now some are missing, either due to them flying away or them being captured. However, a few have died."

The group was in uproar as everyone talked over one another.

"Those poor creatures!"

"What kind of monsters would kill innocent people and animals?"

"What are we going to do?"

"The elders and I," he started cutting many off, "are going to hold a meeting immediately to discuss further action. We will let you know what happens next. For now if your home is in decent enough conditions, please let those whose homes are ruined stay with you."

Everyone nodded in agreement before sadly walking away. Luca turned to me. "Would you like to come to the meeting?"

I shook my head. "No, I'm just going to stay back and help everyone." His eyes lingered on me for a moment as if he was deciding if he should stay or not. "Go, I'll be fine. I've got Esther," I assured him.

He nodded, then ran to the meeting space that sat in front of the rising sun.

"A natural-born leader," Esther said.

"You think so?"

"Oh yes, his mother had that same take-charge attitude. It served her well. He must be sure of his decision."

Part of me couldn't believe that he actually went through with it. He seemed so adamant about not taking the leadership role. I guess circumstances pushed him into it anyways. I followed Esther around as she gave orders to others, doing small tasks she needed assistance with.

"I know this is a hard time for everyone, but we cannot let them just lay here," she explained to a man weeping over his wife. "She deserves a proper burial."

The man sniffled and reluctantly stood. Wiping his face with his forearm, he went with the rest of the men to dig graves. She looked over and gave me a small smile.

"Go to my house and find a big blue vase with oil inside of it."

"Where is it?"

"It should be on the table near the back."

I ran to the house and looked around. Esther's house had to have the least amount of damage. But as I looked over at the table and grabbed the oil, I remembered something. Peto. In the chaos,

I'd completely forgotten my Peto. I set the oil back down and began to frantically look for him. And then I saw him. His white body bright around the dark ash of the singed wall. I picked up my poor friend and held him close. He was gone. Tears escaped my eyes as I gently put him around my neck before grabbing the oil and walking back.

"What's wrong, Ora?" she asked before she looked at Peto. "You poor thing. I'm so sorry. Here let me see him. I'll bury him as well." She gracefully took him from me and laid his body on a cloth and covered him with the other end. I handed her the oil she asked for, and she thanked me. She poured some oil on her hands and, one by one, drew a cross on their foreheads. When she was done, she bowed her head and said a prayer.

"Heavenly Father, we thank you for all that you've done. Even though this is a sad day, we thank you for your grace and mercy. We humbly ask that you forgive these souls any transgression and have mercy upon them. Touch the hearts and souls that are left here to grieve. Give them comfort, Lord. In Jesus's name, amen."

"Amen," others echoed around her. The men had returned from digging and now were carrying body after body followed by the family who wished to plot something in remembrance to their lost loved one.

"What kind of oil is that?"

"It's blessed oil." I frowned. "It's oil that has been prayed over."

"Oh, I get it, I understand now." She turned and drew a cross on me and prayed for me. "Thank you." I smiled. She smiled and touched my shoulder.

Once everyone was buried, we all took a moment to wash ourselves and change if we could. By the time we finished, Luca and the elders returned. Everyone gathered as they stood in front of the space the bodies had once been. Luca looked over at Esther and gave a thankful nod.

"At some point in time, I will be leaving to find those who have wronged us." He glanced over at me. "But for now, we will focus on rebuilding and getting things back to normal or as normal as they can be."

Luca stepped back, and Elijah moved forward. "We have all lost someone, so moving forward will be difficult. But by God's grace, we will make it and be happy once again." Everyone nodded in unison. After a collective prayer, everyone dispersed to sort through their homes for anything that could be salvaged. Luca walked over and pulled me aside.

"How are you doing?"

"I'm okay, but Peto died," I told him, my eyes filled with tears.

"I'm sorry."

I shook my head. "It's my fault. I should've had him with me. I'd been leaving him alone so much since we got here." I wiped tears away with the back of my hand. "So when are you leaving?" I asked, changing the subject.

"We are leaving once everything is settled here."

"We?"

"Of course you're coming with me. I can't leave my best friend all by herself." I smiled, grateful that he thought of me.

"Thanks. So how did the meeting go?"

"Well, I told them I'd be interim chief until they could get someone to take the position."

"Who do you think could?"

"Esther," he stated obviously. When I thought of how she took charge of everyone and got stuff done, it made sense.

"Do you think she would?"

He shrugged. "Maybe, I hope so. Hey, could you help me with something?" I nodded and followed him as he started up the road.

We ended back in the cave he took me to our first day here. He told me to wait outside as he called for Destiny. After a while, he came back.

"She's not here," he told me, running a hand over his face.

"Where do you think she's gone?" I asked, worried. I hoped she'd just flown away when those men came.

"Hopefully she went to the next mountain over. She wasn't one of the ones killed, but I hate to think she may have been captured." He gave a heavy sigh, closing his eyes. I walked over and gave him a hug. With everything that went on last night, I knew he was beyond stressed and in need of it. He smiled and threw his arm over my shoulder as we walked back to the village.

"There needs to be order for us to rebuild as quickly as possible. We will divide into teams. You three…" Esther was instructing people on what to do. I thought about what Luca had said about her maybe taking over, and the more I watched her, the more it made sense. We joined a group and began helping rebuild. Our group was in charge of clearing out the debris so that any damaged parts of the homes would be fixed. Hours had passed, and I was sweeping the last pile of rubble outside when Elijah found me.

"May I speak with you a moment?" he asked in his low, gruff voice. I nodded and followed him aways before he stopped and turned to look at me.

"Forgive me, but in my old age, my memory sometimes leaves me. What was your name again?"

"Ora."

"Is that short for something?" he asked.

"It's short for Alora."

"Ahhh, God's light. Interesting." He looked at me quizzically for a moment. "Walk with an old man."

We slowly began to walk in silence until my curiosity got the best of me.

"You said you wanted to talk to me about something?"

"Yes, I do. I've been around for a long time, and in that time, I've seen some things. Some people around here call me a prophet, although I just like to think that God just likes talking to me." His lips cracked into a smile. "In all my years, I've never seen a spirit like yours."

"Like mine?" I asked, my brow furrowing.

He nodded slowly. "Yes, like yours. This world is full of people with gifts and powers, but what you possess is something greater. More…of God," he said, trying to find the words. "I believe you will do great things, but in order to do so, you must learn to listen to Him."

"Who? Luca?"

He shook his head. "The one who will tell you who you are and what you will have to become in order to save those you love." I looked at him, confused. "You'll see."

After a while of talking to him, I was even more confused than before. Yet he ignored my questions and told me to just be *alert* so I could know when I came in contact with Him. Whatever that meant. We ended up at his house, and he thanked me for talking with him, then ducked inside. I walked back to Esther and Luca thinking about what he said. When I arrived, they were in a heated argument.

"He did what?"

"Lower your voice. You may be chief, but I am still your elder." She seethed through her teeth.

"I apologize." She nodded, and he continued, "How do you know it was him?"

"I may be old, but I know the movements and sound of my son's voice. Why do you think my house is the most untouched? I found him just staring at it. *Mtoto mpumbavu.*" She sucked her teeth. I don't know what *mtoto mpumbavu* meant, but the way she said it, it made me think she insulted her son.

"Well, where does he live now?"

"If I knew, I would have said something. I haven't spoken to him since Nebu died. The last I knew he was in the next town over."

"The only two towns around here are Cauldron and Eryn."

"Cauldron, it was definitely Cauldron." Luca nodded coolly.

"Once we leave, I'm definitely going to look him up."

She grunted and walked away. Luca caught me up on what they were discussing, and I nodded knowingly.

"Yeah, I saw him on his animal thing just staring at her. It was really creepy," I told him. Thinking back, I began to think of the way she looked after he left. That pained look on her face. Guess now I know why.

*****

It was now late, and I was beginning to get tired. We'd managed to clear all of the debris away, but everything else was not finished.

Houses laid in the grass charred and disorganized while the groves were straightened out. We decided to fix the houses with the least amount of damage so we could allow all those with ruined homes to stay with them. Aside from the houses, things didn't look too bad, but the row of crosses scarred the once beautiful field of flowers at the end of the village.

We held a community dinner. Everyone brought some food that I could not pronounce but tasted delicious. After dinner, we all went to the field of flowers. The night air was cool and calm as fireflies buzzed through the air. The low murmur of cries and whispered prayers filled the atmosphere as we all gathered around the gravesites. Elijah walked into the middle of the crowd and lit a lantern before releasing it into the air. The rectangular lantern had a hand-painted flame in the middle that glowed from the candle inside of it. Everyone else released their lanterns into the night sky as a symbol for the ones whose souls were now crossing the spiritual realm. Afterward, we all hugged and talked before dispersing. I was saying good night when Adara walked up to me. As we hugged, I felt her body shaking from crying.

"Are you okay?" I asked her, pulling back.

"My husband died in the attack," she told me as fresh tears welled into her eyes. My own eyes teared up as I hugged her again.

"I'm so sorry, Adara." For a moment, we hugged as she cried, and I cried for her. But soon the moment ended, and she quickly pulled away. Wiping her face with her forearm, she said a brief good-bye and quickly walked away. My heart went out to her. I could only imagine what she was feeling right now. I was watching her walk away with her small children, and I felt a hand on my shoulder. I glanced at Luca before turning again to stare after Adara.

"Hey, are you okay?" I reached up and placed my hand over his.

"I'm okay," I replied. I turned around and gave him a hug. I could guess how she may be feeling. He hugged me back and kissed my forehead.

"Are you ready to go?"

I nodded, and he walked me back to Esther's house. I said good night and was about to go inside when he stopped me.

"Ora?" I looked up at him from the doorway. "I'm so sorry."

"For what?"

"For leaving you in the heat of the battle. I should've taken you with me." I gave him a small smile.

"I told you it's okay."

He reached out and grabbed my hand. "It's not. I promise I'll never leave you again." He looked me in the eyes. I nodded, and he slowly dropped my hands before placing his own in his pockets.

"We'll probably be leaving sometime next week from the looks of things," he paused then spoke again. "I'll let you get to bed, good night."

I hugged him. "Good night, and don't worry, I'm okay." He hugged me tightly before walking down the road to his house. I went inside and changed into my nightclothes. Next week seemed closer than I thought. Argo had become my home these past few weeks, and I was reluctant to leave. But Luca needed me, so I had to go. Esther was already asleep and snoring, so I quietly lay in my bed and closed my eyes.

*****

"I can't believe you're leaving already. You just got here," Esther cried, eyes crinkled and sparkling with tears.

"I know, but we'll be back." She pulled me in for the twentieth hug, this one extra tight. "I'll miss you too," I told her as she finally released me. Luca dropped our bags in front of her before pulling her in for a hug.

"You be good. Keep Ora close to you. She's a special girl."

"I will, I promise."

She looked sad as she gave us one last look-over before she walked inside of her house. Luca pulled the bags over his shoulder and looked at me. "You ready?" I nodded. We got in the car and settled in. We couldn't walk because Esther said, and I quote, "You are insane if you think you're going to walk to Cauldron. It'll take an entire year." So she decided to give us her car since she rarely ever leaves the village. It was a small blue car with black leather seats.

Seeing how much Luca had to squeeze to get into the driver's side was beyond entertaining. He pulled a lever and pushed the seat back so that his legs wouldn't stop him from turning the wheel.

"You look like a giant in this car." I chuckled.

"It's way too cramped in this car," he groaned as he adjusted everything. I laughed and shook my head. Poor guy, this car was made for Esther, a five-foot old woman, not all six feet of Luca.

Eventually he figured everything out, and we started on the road.

The trip took a few hours, and the longer we drove, the more I understood why we couldn't just walk. We were now driving along a narrow road that scaled the side of a mountain. It was a one-way road, but it still made me nervous, as if we were soon to fall down the side and to our demise. Luca glanced at me and put his hand on mine.

"It's okay, don't be nervous. Just don't look out the window." I nodded and looked down at my hands. They were shaking, so that didn't help. I reached into the side of my backpack and grabbed the flower that was there. I twisted it around in my fingers, amazed at how it was still alive, only slightly wilted. Luca glanced at me before looking back at the road.

"What's that?" he asked as he turned down a road that led off the mountain.

"The flower that guy gave me back in that town. Remember?" I asked. He'd been so upset when he saw him flirting with me.

"How could I forget?" He snorted, "You're too friendly, you know."

"Is that a bad thing?" I looked up at him.

"No, I mean just in the case of strangers. Something could have happened to you."

"Well, you were a stranger," I pointed out.

"I...hmm, point taken." I looked back down at my flower as it sparkled in the sunlight. Then I remembered something.

"Luca?"

"Yes?"

"How did he make this flower?"

"What do you mean?"

"The guy. When we were at the table, he closed his hand, and the flower grew out of his palm"—I demonstrated—"then he just plucked it and gave it to me."

He was quiet for a moment. "He's a chlorokinetic," he told me matter-of-factly.

"What's that?"

"It means he can manipulate nature. Like plants and stuff. That's how he made the flower appear in his hand."

What does he mean appear? I looked down at my flower. It seemed real and even smelled real; it was just so sparkly. I knew all plants weren't like this because the ones in Argo were green.

"So this is fake?"

"No, it's a real flower."

"The flowers in Argo don't look like this though."

"It's a special flower from a different place."

"From where, though?" I pressed. For some reason, I felt like I've seen it before.

"I'd tell you if I knew." My shoulders fell. "I'm sorry."

"It's okay…does everyone have powers?" I asked curiously.

"I believe so."

"What are yours?" I turned to face him, and he smiled.

"Pyrokinetics"—he looked over at me—"basically fire." It all made sense. The dragons, the flames I saw when he was fighting, I wasn't imagining it.

"Do I have powers?"

"I'm not entirely sure. I've never met anyone that didn't," he added when he saw my face.

I turned back around, slumped in my chair. What was my gift? Could I even do anything amazing like throwing fire or growing flowers in my hand? I sighed heavily and looked out the window.

*****

We arrived in Cauldron a little before sunset. The sun was low in the sky casting shades of orange and red and hues of purple and pink.

To say that the city was big was an understatement. It was encased by a giant wall and an iron door. The buildings sat high in the sky as the inhabitants bustled below. The street was filled with traffic as a loud crowd walked in two separate directions in a rush. The car crawled in traffic as passersby moved in between the cars. A giant clock could be seen some feet ahead of us as it clanged loudly at the top of the hour. Street shops surrounded the roads, all different and selling their specialties—from shoe repairs to a bakery that sat beside a blacksmith and a salon across from a hat shop and a general store. Sick of traffic, Luca pulled into a spot in front of the general store and got out. He came around, opening my door. I stepped into the humid air and immediately started sweating. And I thought it was hot in Argo. Luca locked the door as he held the door to the general store open for me. I walked into the quaint store that was lined with wooden shelves. Shelves in the middle created an aisle in-between, making the store look almost like a library, but instead of books, the shelves housed a variety of foods and drinks and personal items.

"Good morning," an elderly man greeted warmly from behind the counter. I smiled and greeted him back before wandering through the aisles. Everything was neatly shelved and organized by food items, just like books. I grabbed some food and a drink before heading to the counter to wait for Luca.

"Hello, young lady," the cashier said with a smile.

"Hello." I smiled back. "I absolutely love this store. It reminds me of a library."

"I'll let my wife know you love it." A small dimple appeared in his left cheek. He was a tall older gentleman who wore wire-rimmed spectacles over his gray eyes. His face was unshaven with gray hairs that peppered through his red-haired beard. His hair was curly at the top, the sides cut short. He reached a freckled hand to his throat as he cleared it, adjusting his tie in the process. A bright yellow band with a black design was on his left finger.

"May I see your wedding ring?" I asked. He laid his hand flat on the counter for me to see. The black design turned out to be cursive. He turned it so I could read what it said. "Mea usque ad extremum spiritum." I didn't even attempt to pronounce it, afraid of butchering it.

"Until my last breath," he translated. "It's Latin."

"Wow," I replied, continuing to stare at the ring. The cursive was etched in gold, making the words almost glow. "How long have you guys been married?"

"Forty-two years. Every year has been better than the last," he added. "Do you like books?" he asked, changing the subject as he folded his hands together.

"I do." He handed me a business card. "My wife owns the library up the street. You should check it out when you have a chance."

I gratefully took the card, excited to go. Alonso always brought me books to read, but I'd never been in a library. I only knew about the shelves from the pictures he'd show me. He'd take pictures of everything so I could experience it from my cell. I missed him so much. Luca finally came to the counter and placed his things beside mine. My eyes widened at the amount.

"You are one hungry guy." The cashier laughed.

"It's been a long day, and we haven't eaten in a while," he replied, pulling out his wallet. We'd gone through the food Esther had given us at the beginning of the trip.

"Well, if you like, you two could join my wife and I for dinner tonight," he offered. Luca looked up at him suspiciously.

"I don't know..." he said hesitantly.

"Please, Luca? I'm sure whatever his wife is cooking is way better than fruit snacks and potato chips," I begged.

"All right," he finally said.

"I'm closing up in a couple hours. You can just head to the library. I'll let my wife know you're coming," he told us. We nodded, and he checked us out. We went back to the car and put the bags in the trunk.

"Ora, you can't just go around to everyone's house. Some people are dangerous." He scolded once inside.

"Does he look dangerous to you?" I asked.

"That's not the point"

"Okay, I hear you. But I don't think he's bad. I have a good feeling about him."

"I hope you're right."

We took a short ride up the street to the library. It was a tall old building with huge white columns. Library was engraved into a plaque in the center. As we walked in, I inhaled deeply. It smelled of dirt and paper with a hint of vanilla as if someone had sprayed a freshener. It was significantly bigger on the inside with high vaulted ceilings edged with planks. The shelves were tall and solid wood like the ones in the convenience store we'd just left. There was a big half-moon-shaped desk that glistened with polish directly across from the door. There, an older woman stood, smiling sweetly, her hands folded atop the desk.

"Hello, honey, how may I help you?" her voice was calm like a patient mother's. She wore a collared dress with a ribbon tie tied underneath. Her thick red cardigan was draped over her shoulder as if she'd been in the process of putting it on before we came in. She had wide purple eyes like mine that were framed with now graying eyelashes. Her hair was curly tied in a chignon at the nape of her neck as curls hung loose around her head. Faint traces of a red lipstick were on her lips like it'd been rubbed off until a cup she was drinking. The closer I walked, the bigger her smile got.

"Hello, a man from the convenience store sent us here to find his wife?" As soon as I said it, I realized that I never caught his name.

"Ah, you're the ones Gabriel told me about." She looked over at Luca, then turned back to me, smiling.

"Yes, you must be his wife."

"Nice to meet you. I am Seraph."

"I'm Ora," I told her. She had the nicest smile. I couldn't help but smile back.

"Luca," he introduced himself, looking around

She nodded. "Ora and Luca. Well, if you can just give me fifteen minutes, I'll get my things, and we can head to the house."

"Yes, of course, take your time. I wanted to look around anyways." She looked at me curiously before a smile cracked through her lips.

"That's fine. Just use the scanner to check out anything you want to take with you," with that, she walked away, her kitten heels clicking against the stone floor.

I eagerly headed into the direction of books, fingering each one carefully. Their hardened spines enclosed worlds unknown, worlds waiting to be discovered by me. I was so happy I was practically bouncing.

"I didn't know you liked books," Luca commented in a low voice.

"I've loved them since I was a kid. Alonso would read to me every night. He said even though I couldn't go anywhere didn't mean I couldn't travel." I smiled sadly at the thought of him.

"He read to me too," he replied quietly. After a moment, he grabbed a book off the shelf. "What about this?"

I looked at the book and made a face. "Shakespeare? No, thank you."

"What's wrong with it?" He laughed.

"For one, almost all of his stuff ends in tragedy, it's sad."

"Tragedy is supposed to be sad," he pointed out.

"True, but I for one do not like sad endings. I prefer the couple stays together."

"You're an eternal optimist. Most relationships end in tragedy." He put the book back in the open spot.

"I refuse to believe that." He smirked but said nothing else. One after another, I picked it up and read the back, putting it in a pile or back on the shelf. By the time our fifteen minutes was up, I'd created an impressive small pile of books. Luca carried them to the checkout counter and checked them out for me as Mrs. Sera walked up with bags in hand.

"Ready?" she asked.

We both nodded. I grabbed my books off the counter, and Luca carried her bags for her. We helped her into her car, then got in ours to follow her. After a while, we pulled into a stone driveway that led up to a lovely two-story home. Like the library, the front had two large columns, one on each side of the porch. A set of rocking chairs and a bench swing were nestled on either side of the bright-blue door surrounded by beautiful flowers. We got out of the car and followed her up to the house. The walkway was lined with an array of flowers and planters before reaching the flower bushes in front of the porch. She opened the front door and walked inside. The entryway was beyond immaculate. A thick artisan rug was laid across the marble floors. The walls were a light shade of blue that was highlighted by the lovely painting that sat above a table. The hallway was long as we walked down, passing a couple equally impressive rooms. We settled in a sitting room. I sat in a cushy pink chair, and Luca sat in the matching one across from me. She asked if we wanted anything to drink or snacks before excusing herself. She came back with a tray full of different drinks and food items and placed it on the huge coffee table in the center before sitting on the blue sofa next to my chair. She crossed her legs at the ankles and placed her hands in her lap.

"So you must tell me about yourselves. How did you come to be in Cauldron?" Luca told her about the massacre in Argo and how he found out that the culprit was in Cauldron. She nodded as she listened and made looks of horror as he detailed what happened.

"I am so sorry, sweetheart. I can only imagine the pain and immense pressure you are under." Luca nodded. "I can't imagine why anyone would even do that."

"The elders and I believed it was a distraction so that they could take the dragons. They killed some and possibly took others while they attacked us."

"Those poor creatures." She shook her head sadly. "Are you from there as well?" she asked me.

"No, ma'am. I don't actually know where I'm from."

She opened her mouth to speak but was interrupted by the sound of the door closing. "Honey? Are they here? Where are you guys?" her husband called from the entryway.

"In the sitting room, love," she called back.

He came in through the open archway, smiling. "Hey guys. What's up?" he asked before reaching onto the tray and grabbing something to eat.

"We were just talking. I'll go start dinner. Ora, would you like to help me?"

"Yes, but I don't know how much help I'll be," I told her, standing.

"Nonsense." She looped her arm in mine and led me to the kitchen.

*****

As Luca finished his last bite, I could tell that he didn't regret coming. The food was immaculate, all thanks to Seraph. I only chopped miscellaneous things for her while she cooked. She insisted it was a big help. I watched as she and Gabriel spoke to each other, smiling and laughing, and wondered if this was what it was like to grow up with parents. I looked down at my hands wondering if I'd ever get to experience it. Luca caught my eye and gave me a small smile as if he knew what I was thinking. Eventually we all settled back into the sitting room with our tea.

"Ora, you mentioned earlier that you don't know where you're from?" Seraph asked.

"Yes, I did," I replied, putting my cup down, "it's a long story."

"Well, I'd love to hear it sometime." She smiled as if she figured it was a lot. To suddenly spill your entire life out to someone you just met, I didn't even know how to start, let alone if I even should.

"Well—"

"Ora." Luca gave me a look, and I read it immediately. He didn't want me to feel pressured to tell her. It's my story; I get to decide who I tell it to and when.

"It's okay," I turned to face Seraph. "I was separated from mother when I was younger. I was too young to remember much of where we were from."

Her hand raised to her mouth. "I am so sorry, dear."

"It's okay, I've been fortunate to find people who care about me." Luca reached over and squeezed my hand.

"Yes, that is a blessing. The Lord works in mysterious ways," she stared at me for a moment but said nothing else.

"So where will you two be staying?" Gabriel interjected. Up until now, he'd been sitting comfortably in his chair, nursing his tea.

"We're not entirely sure yet. Are there any hotels you'd recommend?"

He snorted. "These hotels here are not the safest. Rooms are broken into more often than not. You can stay here."

"We don't want to impose."

"Nonsense." He stood up, teacup in hand. "Come with me. I'll show you the room."

Luca followed Gabriel, bags in hand, leaving Seraph and I alone. "Honey, have you noticed we look somewhat similar?"

"Yeah, I have…"

"We have the same lavender eyes, and judging from your locks, I'd say curly hair as well."

"You're not…" I trailed off.

"Oh no, my dear. I'm too old to be your mother."

She quickly reassured me. My face fell ever so slightly.

"There's a place called Arcadia where the people look a lot like you and me." My eyebrows raised. "People with our eye color are called Arcadians. That's where you're from."

"How are you so sure?" How did she know that right off the bat?

"We're the only ones with eyes like ours. Each region has their own distinctive traits. Have you noticed in Argo everyone has eyes like Luca's?"

They did in fact. I'd noticed it but thought it to be merely a coincidence or something due to them being close to a volcano.

Luca walked in before I could ask her more.

"I'll let you two get some sleep. We can talk more tomorrow." I nodded and watched as she walked away. Trying to process this information would make sleeping nearly impossible. Eventually I followed Luca to the bedroom. I opened the glittery door to reveal another magnificent part of the house. In the middle of the huge room were two canopy beds pushed against the wall, draped with white linen. The room was painted a soft cream and blue. Floor-length windows disturbed the extensive wall to the right, a desk and two chairs centered between them. The carpet was lush and covered with a thick blue rug near the bed. The room was rather empty aside from some dressers and nightstands that were strategically placed around the room and a few paintings. A light fixture near the floor cast a low light that immediately made me relax. The more I looked around, the more it looked like a child's room.

"Do they have children?" Luca shrugged. I made a note to ask them tomorrow. My bag rested on the side with the big windows, marking that it was mine. I grabbed my clothes and changed in the attached bathroom. It was a brightly lit room with a huge tub in the center. A walk-in shower was to the right of it and the double vanity to the left. I brushed my teeth and washed my face. *Arcadia,* I thought. *So that's where I'm from.* The more I thought of it, the more hopeful I became. Maybe I'd find my mother after all.

I pulled my hair into a bun and went back into the bedroom. Moonlight flooded through the windows, casting long shadows off the beds. As I lay under the covers, I turned and faced Luca who to my surprise was wide-awake.

"Can't sleep?" I asked, snuggling deep into my covers. He shook his head. "She told me I'm from Arcadia," I told him after a moment. His orange eyes softened in the moonlight.

"Seraph?"

"Yes."

"So what are you thinking?"

"I mean, I have so many questions, and I just keep thinking, what if my mom is still alive?"

I saw him nodding.

"Maybe you can talk to her tomorrow and she can tell you more about it," he suggested.

"Yeah, maybe." I closed my eyes and started to feel drowsy.

"Ora?" Luca called after a moment.

"Hmm?"

"Thanks for coming with me." I opened my eyes briefly, then closed them again.

"Of course. You're stuck with me."

His laugh floated to my side of the room. "I love you."

"I love you too," I replied, drifting to sleep.

*****

85

I woke up the next morning to a made bed, and Luca gone. I rubbed the sleep out of my eyes and stretched as I looked around. After realizing he wasn't in the room, I prepared for the day, then went downstairs.

"Good morning, dear," Seraph greeted sweetly. She slid me a cup of coffee and a plate of food across the island from where she stood.

"Sleep well?"

"That bed you gave me was like sleeping on a cloud."

"Well, I'm glad." She laughed.

"Hey, is Luca here?"

"No, he rode into town with Gabriel a while ago. He told me to give you that note there." She nodded to a piece of paper to the right of me.

I left early to get a head-start on my search. I'll be back later. Be safe, I love you.

I folded it back and put it in my back pocket and started to eat my food. Seraph washed the dishes as I ate, giving me time to think. After I finished, I handed her my dishes and just watched her clean them.

"Could you tell me about Arcadia?"

Her lips cracked into a smile. "I'd love to."

"It was a magical place to grow up in. There were a lot of predators, so our homes were high up in the trees. As a child, I remember climbing down the ropes into the lush jungle floor. There were these day lilies that my mother would grow in our yard. They were pink and sparkled in the daylight and smelled so sweet. We weren't as modern as this city was when I was growing up. We had everything we needed, and nothing more. But we were happy." She smiled as she remembered something. "Everything glowed at night because of the phosphorus in the ground and plants. Blues, pinks, purple, every shade you could think of glowed and covered the plants. The color would vibrate when you touched them like ripples in the water."

I reached inside of my backpack and pulled out my flower. "Like this?" She took it carefully and twirled it in her hands.

"Where did you get this?" she asked gently, touching the petals.

"Someone made it for me in a town we stopped in. He called me an omni something."

"Omnikinetic," she told me, handing back my flower. She stood and walked over to a bookshelf and grabbed a book.

"What's an omnikinetic?"

"We are. All Arcadians are." She sat back down beside me with the book. "When I was younger, a man came from the outside. It was very strange because we rarely had any visitors, maybe three in my entire life up to that point. I can't remember his name exactly. I just remember he had eyes of fire. He came and promised to 'modernize us.' People were excited. They'd never seen the things this man had, and they wanted them for themselves. He wanted to know more about us in exchange for the things he brought, so we showed him our powers."

"Our powers?"

"Yes, omnikinetics are very special. We can move anything with just our minds." My brow furrowed. "Here, watch me."

She looked down at the book, and it began to float in the air. It flipped through a few pages before stopping on one.

"I..." I was speechless. She looked at me and smiled, but I couldn't take my eyes off the book. It was just hovering above the table as if the action was natural for it. It slowly moved and stopped in front of me. It had stopped on a page with a picture on it.

"That's Arcadia." I scooted closer as memories flooded back to me all at once.

"I remember." Seraph turned curiously at me. I told her about what happened as a child, my mother being taken from me.

She nodded slowly. "Yes, I remember that time. So many of us were killed. Rulers from the other villages kidnapped so many of us and killed off the rest."

"But why?"

"They craved our power. They wanted to control it and use it to conquer other lands. When we didn't go willingly, they kidnapped some and killed others. There was so much chaos, so I ran and I found this place and Gabriel." She smiled ruefully. "I'm sorry about your mother."

"It's okay. I know she's alive. I just have to find her."

Seraph nodded. "I'll help in any way I can." The book floated back down and gently laid on the table.

"The Great Separation desolated Arcadia. So many were taken, so many families were torn apart. It's rare that I've seen another one. I haven't seen an Arcadian since I left." Her eyes lowered to the ground, deep in thought.

I reached out and touched her hand. "Well, I'm glad I've found you."

She smiled and patted my hand. "As am I. Now let's get ready to go. I'll have to open the library soon." We stood and headed outside to the car.

*****

I sat between two bookshelves, cradling a book in my lap. I was deeply involved with the tragedy of Romeo and Juliet when someone stood near me, casting a shadow over me.

"Ahem," a deep voice cleared. I looked up squinting at the bright fluorescents. This tall man wore a long burnt-orange coat that covered his suit underneath. His eyes were the same color as his jacket, the same color as Luca's. I pulled my feet to my chest and out of his way.

"Thank you," he murmured as he walked past. My gaze followed him as he walked out of the aisle and down the hall toward the door. Something about him was vaguely familiar. As I muddled over who this tall stranger was, I gathered my things into my bag and pulled it over my shoulder. I strode over to the front desk and found Seraph stamping books from the drop-off box.

"Hey, did you see the guy that just walked out of here?" I placed my stuff on the counter and pointed over my shoulder.

"Can't say I did." She looked up at me over the brim of her glasses. "Why, was he bothering you?"

"No, I just feel like I've seen him before." I turned and looked at the door even though he was long gone. Where did I see him? "Do you need help with anything?" I asked, coming around the desk.

"You know I'm starting to love you." She smiled and bumped my shoulder. I smiled back and started on the large stack to her right.

*****

"Did you know that many believe Arcadians came from heaven?" Seraph mentioned on the car ride home. We'd just locked up the library for the night and were headed back to the house for dinner and a much-needed shower.

"Angels?"

She nodded. "Yes. People believe that God saw all of the wrong in the world that he sent down some angels to help mankind. That's why out of all the areas, we have the most powers."

"Wow."

"It's just a story. I personally don't believe it," she offered with a smile.

I pondered over the idea as we rode home. We pulled into the driveway to see Gabriel arguing with a police officer. We hopped out and walked over.

"What's going on?" Seraph asked as she grabbed Gabriel's arm to calm him.

"They're taking Luca."

"What?" we both exclaimed. I went over to the police car and looked in the glass. Luca was sitting in the dark with his hands behind his back and his head low. I banged on the glass, but he didn't bother looking at me. From the blue siren lights, all I could see was a look of pure anger as his jaw worked.

"Ma'am, please step away from the vehicle," the officer told me as he moved toward me. I took a step back.

"But what did he do?"

"Trespassing on private property."

"But that doesn't mean you have to arrest him," I replied, getting upset.

"He broke the law. This is the consequence for his actions. Now if you would excuse me." He opened the driver door and slid in. He shut it closed in front of my dumbfounded face. He was taking Luca from me, the only person I had in the world.

"Please don't take him. Please!" I begged, banging on his window. He ignored me and looked over his shoulder as he backed out of the driveway. I fell to my knees and cried. I had absolutely no one.

CHAPTER

A few days had passed since they took Luca. Life seemed to become more unbearable as each new day passed. It felt as if I was back in my cell alone and just waiting for anyone to come and help me. My breathing was shallow, and my heartbeat was pained with each pulse of my blood. All I wanted to do was scream.

"Ora darling?" Seraph called softly as she knocked on the other side of the door. I'd secluded myself in my room since he left, just sleeping on his bed and crying.

"Ora, honey, please open up," she asked sympathetically. I felt bad for making her worry so much, but I couldn't bring myself to get out of bed. Why did God keep taking people away from me?

I heard a jingle of keys and the click of the door unlocking. I guess they found the spare key. The sound of her kitten heels were muffled against the carpet as she came over to me.

"Honey." She rubbed my back through the sheets. She smelled of warm honey and flowers like she always did, and her warm hand melted my hard exterior. She pulled the sheets from over me and laid my head on her lap as she stroked my hair.

"Shh, it's okay," she cooed as I cried. She hummed a song and handed me a tissue. She didn't tell me to get over it or to stop pouting. She just let me be sad, and it honestly made me feel better.

"I'm sorry," I apologized, sniffling as I looked down at her ruined dress now wet with tears and snot.

"It can be washed." She waved her hand dismissively. "Talk to me. How are you feeling right now?"

"I just don't understand. Why does God keep taking people from me?" I blurted as I wiped slowly at the tears that came out too fast.

"My mom, now Luca? I don't know why he keeps doing this to me. You told me he would make everything better, but it's not. It's only worse." I was upset. I'd given my life to him and now all of this?

She pulled me into a hug. "If you never had a problem, how would you know God could fix it?" she replied simply.

"I never thought of it like that." I swiped at my eyes. She had a point, I admit, but it didn't make me feel any better.

"Just have faith. He'll be back before you know it." I nodded. "Now let's get you some food," she said as my stomach growled. She held me close and walked us downstairs. I repeated her words, *Just have faith. He'll be back before you know it.* He'll be back before you know it.

*****

I woke up with a jolt, my heart racing. Perspiration dripped into my eyes as I gathered my bearings. This one was slightly different. My mom had hurried into a closet after hiding me just before a guard kicked open the door, splitting the doorframe to bits. Their heavy breathing seemed amplified through their masks. They rummaged through our things, throwing photos and furniture every which way. A lamp rose from the table and crashed into the back of their heads, sending them to the ground. My mother rushed over to the closet and pulled me out before grabbing my hand to run out the door.

I rubbed my eyes and turned on the lamp beside me, casting a comforting glow on the dark room. I wrapped myself tighter in the sheets and prayed, begging God to stop these dreams from coming.

CHAPTER

Almost a month had passed since I saw Luca. Each day dragged on, but with the help of Seraph and Gabriel, it was more bearable. She continued to teach me how to use my powers as a distraction. I was more than grateful for it.

"Now it is important that you understand that you cannot let your anger or sadness or any negative emotion drive your omnikinetics," she instructed.

"Why what will happen?" I asked curiously. She tilted her head and looked at me.

"Come with me." I followed her outside and to the car where she proceeded to get in. I stood at the door staring at her. "Come on, get in." she cranked up the car.

We drove a little ways down the road until we came to a wooded area. She turned the car off and walked into the woods.

"Uh, where are we going?" I asked cautiously. It was nearing sunset, and the woods looked thick, an easy place to get lost. She ignored my question and came back to grab my hand. We walked until we came to a clearing, and she stopped in the middle of it. She let my hand go and walked to the edge.

"Scream!" she yelled.

"What?" I could barely hear her over the wind that made my teeth slightly chatter.

"Scream! Let it all out," she told me again.

I took a deep breath and screamed, and with it, I let out everything I was feeling. I opened my eyes and jumped at the sight. Above me was a million needles made of bark. They froze in the air as if floating statues. Sharp little swords poised over the clearing. I looked over at Seraph who had her hands up. She stopped it. With a quick motion of her hands, the needles rose high into the sky and formed into a ball, which she set gently down on the other side of the clearing. She walked over to me and smiled.

"That's why."

"I'm so sorry I—" She waved her hand, cutting me off.

"*Psh*, that's nothing. Your emotions determine how your omni-kinetics work. With negative emotions, negative things happen. Your anger and grief ripped the bark from the trees and made them daggers. Kind of like the way they ripped Luca from you."

I plopped onto the ground and looked around at the stripped-down trees surrounding the clearing.

"You have to be careful. You cannot let fear or anger get the better of you," she added after a moment. I nodded. I knew she was right; it was just mind-blowing to see. Still dumbfounded, she helped me up and looped her arm through mine as we walked back to the car.

"I'm glad I brought you out here. You would have broken all of the windows in my house." She laughed.

*****

When we got home, I ran up the stairs to change into something warmer. I was imagining the warmth I'd feel wrapped in that wool blanket on my bed as I opened the door.

There he was. Sitting on the bed, taking off his boots. I stood in the doorway staring at him. His hair was longer now with bits of fluff and leaves poking out of it. His clothes were dirty with stains and dirt marks all over his once white shirt. A red puffy scar peeked from under his shirt as he slouched down to place a boot on the floor. He looked up and gave me a small smile.

"Hey, Ora."

I ran over and hugged him. He was warmer than usual, which I found odd considering the temperature outside. What was really odd was the way he hugged me back. I clung to his neck, pressed against him, but his arms felt loose around me. It was a change from his usual bear hugs. I pulled back and looked at him.

"I missed you so much," I told him, tears pricking my eyes. He wiped the one stray tear with his thumb and pulled me into a slightly tighter hug.

"I missed you too," he mumbled into my hair. He held me for a second as he stroked my hair before finally pulling away. "I'm going to go shower." He grabbed his clothes and walked into the bathroom, locking the door behind him. I sat on my bed and looked at his clothes. He'd clearly been through a lot, and judging by his clothes, I'm not sure he was going to tell me about it.

*****

Dinner was silent, except the sound of clinking silverware against the plates as we pushed our food around. Luca hadn't spoken since he'd gotten out the shower. He moved methodically, as if he was a machine performing its normal functions and duties. He sat quietly at the end of the table slowly eating his dinner as he stared at the plate. His head may have been low, but I could feel a heaviness around him, almost as if he was angry. Gabriel, Seraph, and I had all made failed attempts at getting him to talk. From asking him how he liked the food to being glad that he was finally home, but he didn't budge. He just continued staring at his plate and eating in silence. Once he was done, he stood and took his dishes to the sink, washed them, and went up the stairs. Seraph and I stared at each other as we listened to the sound of the door closing lightly in the distance. I let out a heavy sigh.

"Just give him time." Seraph patted my hand before taking our plates to the sink. Gabriel looked at me and quickly looked down.

"He's been through a great ordeal, Ora. You must be patient with him," he advised knowingly.

My eyes narrowed. "What happened to him?"

Gabriel looked toward the kitchen and ducked his head back at me. "She'd kill me if I told you."

"Sure would. It's not your business to tell," she agreed as she passed us dessert.

"He told you what happened?" I was a bit hurt that Luca would confide in him before he did me.

He shook his head. "I can read minds," he told me as he stuffed his face with chocolate cake.

"What! You're psychic and you didn't tell me?" He looked up at me as he swallowed. "So you know what happened then. Tell me."

"It's really not my business to tell." He wiped his mouth, looking at Seraph who gave him a warning look.

"Just talk to him in the morning. Maybe he'll be more willing to open up," Seraph told me as she ate a spoonful of her dessert. I agreed with a heavy sigh. As much as I wanted to know what was plaguing my best friend, I knew pressuring him wouldn't be the best way to go about it. So I just ate my cake and thought of how to get him to talk in the morning.

*****

We woke up around the same time the next morning. It was still early, the sun barely peeking through the clouds. Luca immediately threw on some sweatpants and a hoodie. He was tying his shoes as he watched me pull my hair into a ponytail. I slept in my sweatpants, eager to catch him before he went on his morning run, not wanting to risk him leaving before I got dressed. We left the house and headed to the pond area that wasn't far up the street. I mentioned how beautiful it was this morning, but of course, he was still silent. The morning air was crisp, and there was a slight wind that chilled me through my jacket. We ran in silence for a while before we slowed to a walk to cool down.

"Luca, please talk to me." We had been walking for a while now, and every question I asked, he dodged in some way or another.

"There's nothing to say, Ora." He sighed. I reached out and grabbed his arm to stop him from walking. My legs burned as I tried to keep up with his long stride.

"If it's nothing, then why can't you tell me?" I pressed.

"Because it doesn't concern you!" he snapped. I took a step back. He never spoke to me like that before. He raked a hand through his hair.

"You concern me," I replied quietly.

"Maybe. But this is different. This I have to handle on my own." He started back off on his fast pace. I almost had to run to keep up.

"Let me help you."

"I don't need your help."

"Yes, you do."

"No, I don't." His voice was getting harsher with each response. I almost wished he stayed quiet. His silence hurt less. "I don't want you coming. You'll only get in the way."

"In the way of what?" I questioned. "What are you going to do?"

He grumbled. "Ora, what do you want from me?"

"I want you to talk to me. I want to know what you're thinking."

He spun around his orange eyes glowing with anger. "Do you really want to know what I'm thinking? I know who did it, who destroyed Argo. I'm going to go end it." The severity of his words made my head spin.

"You're going to kill them?" I took a step back and looked at him. This wasn't the Luca I know.

"You asked," he argued. He was shaking with anger, and the more I looked at him, the more he changed before my eyes. My friend no longer had a soft sunset glow in his eyes; they were now hard and steely. His pupils looked sharp as if they were boring holes into your skull. His usually relaxed large frame was radiant with heat and anger. I didn't like it.

"Luca, you can't."

"I can't?" he mocked. "I can't? What about what they did? How they set fire to my home, our home. How they slaughtered countless innocent people who did nothing to deserve a death like that. Who killed and enslaved animals who just wanted to live peacefully. Don't tell me what I can't do. I'm simply doing what's right. It's justice for me and my people."

"Luca, that's not justice," I retorted.

"No? What do you know about justice? Your whole life has been an injustice. Someone dragged you from your home and took your family away. You only know injustice."

I shook my head. "That's not true. God is justice. Let him fight this for you. He knows more than you do." I was trying desperately to make him see. He wasn't thinking clearly.

"I know plenty enough to do this on my own. He can handle them after I'm done." He stalked off.

"I can't believe you said that." He stopped and stared ahead as I looked at his back. He turned back around and looked at me.

"Since when did you become so concerned with what God has to say?" He was being nasty, but I refused to let it get to me.

"Since I got to know him. Murder is not the answer."

"It may not be *the* answer, but it's *my* answer. Those people do not deserve to live after what they've done," he barked.

"Luca—"

"Look, I'm done arguing with you. I wasn't asking for your permission. You wanted to know. Don't get mad now that you do."

"I just don't understand why you think this is the answer."

"Of course, you don't understand. Innocent, naive Ora who has never so much as even killed a fly. You were stuck in a cage your whole life with only Lonso to tell you about the outside world. Ora who was so scared to even step on the grass the first time she saw it. Ora who was so trusting of strangers to just blindly go in their houses right away without a second thought. The little girl who is scared of trouble out of fear of being locked back up in that cage." He was making fun of me out of anger. I knew that; it just did not make it hurt less. His sharp words pierced my heart until it became heavy in my chest. I swallowed over the lump in my throat as tears welled in my eyes. Tears Luca didn't see as he stormed off. I didn't even bother following him.

I'm not sure how long I stood there after he left, but my lips were now numb from the cold. I wrapped my arms around myself and walked back to the house. He wasn't there when I got back. I ran up the stairs to change into something warmer. I pulled on my new lavender sweater that Seraph bought me the other day and sat on my bed. Luca's harsh words rang through my head the longer I sat there. Each one felt like a stab to my heart, dragging it down with each wound. To make matters worse, he ran off, and I had no idea where he was going; but as I looked around the room, I realized he wasn't coming back. I lay my head on my pillow and cried as I prayed. I didn't know what else to do. Everything seemed to be falling apart, and I didn't know how it would get any better.

I must have fallen asleep because when I opened my eyes, the sunlight was slanted as it shined through the window. I went inside the bathroom and splashed cold water on my puffy eyes, trying to look presentable before I went downstairs. When I got down there, Seraph and Gabriel were holding an intense conversation. They spoke in low voices that faded to silence as they saw me walk in. Seraph looked up, and her smile faded when she saw my face.

"What happened?" she asked with a look of concern.

"Luca ran off." They exchanged a quick look.

"Do you know where he went?" Gabriel asked, pulling on his glasses.

I shook my head, and he sighed. He looked at Seraph who gave him a nod, and he cleared his throat.

"Sit, Ora, please." I sat on the sofa across from them and folded my arms. "What did he say before he ran off?"

"Just that he knew who destroyed Argo and he was going to kill them," I explained. Seraph's eyes widened when I said *kill*. She looked as shocked as I was when he said it.

"Yeah, he knows who did it. That's why I didn't want to tell you what I knew last night. It seems he is set on murdering the man."

"Well, can't we just go stop him?" I scooted forward in my seat. The last thing I wanted to do was sit in the house and hope and pray he would come back.

"It's not that simple."

"But it is. You know where he is going, so we can go and stop him before he can do anything," I argued. Why didn't he want to help?

"Ora, you have to understand. Two omnikinetics and a psychic cannot just go bust into someone's domain. Especially not the domain of *that* man." He wasn't making sense to me. Four against one seemed like it would end in our favor.

"What man?"

"The king," Seraph told me with a saddened look.

The king? "Oh my god, he's insane! He's going to get himself killed." I stood up and started pacing. Maybe the king would have mercy on him if he changed his mind. No, that wouldn't work because Luca would never back down. I was working out a million different scenarios that ended with Luca alive when Seraph interrupted my thoughts.

"Ora, we cannot just go to the castle and demand things. As soon as he gets past the guards, if he even gets that far, they will lock him up and throw away the key. King Jasper is not a kind man," she informed me.

"You must also consider who you are. Omnikinetics are very rare and very sought-after. I'm afraid if you and Seraph go, you will only be putting yourselves in danger as well." He was trying to get me to see his point, but I couldn't. I didn't care if I would be in danger; I couldn't let Luca do this.

"It's better if we all just stay and hope for the best."

"No," I stopped, pacing and looked at them, "you stay, I'll go."

"Ora, that's not necessary."

"I can't just wait here and do nothing. I'm going after him."

"If you really want to go, just wait until the morning. Just stay the night, pray about it, and if you feel like that's what you should do, then leave in the morning. We'll even help you get there." I could hear the hesitation in her voice as she spoke. She didn't want me to leave either, but she just wanted me to be sure.

"Sera—" Gabriel started.

"She's dead set on going. There's nothing we can do to stop her, so we might as well help her," she cut him off. He nodded in agreement. I knew they just didn't want anything to happen to me, but I had to go. Something bad was going to happen. I could feel it.

"In the meantime, I want you to come with me. I'll feel better if you have more training under your belt." She stood, and I followed her outside. We stood in the front courtyard to the right of the estate.

I figured she thought this was a safe enough space because it was surrounded with the brick of the house.

"Fight me."

"What?" I looked around wondering who she was talking to.

"Fight me!" she yelled as she sent sticks flying toward me. I twisted my wrists and sent the wood crashing into the brick. Before I could turn, she sent a cloud of leaves toward me. With a quick motion of one hand, I swirled the leaves into a mini tornado and, with the other hand, sent it flying toward her. She swung her arm, causing it to dissipate as quickly as it appeared.

"Not bad."

"Thank y—" suddenly my feet swept up off the ground, and I was flung high into the air. "Agh!"

"Never lose focus. Just because I stopped doesn't mean you let your guard down!" she yelled up to me. She gently lowered me back to the ground. She jogged over to me, smiling. "Good. I want you to remember to always keep your emotions in check. Use them to put power behind each attack," she instructed.

I nodded and threw my hands up. We practiced proper stances and techniques well after the sun went down. The trees cast dark shadows on the clearing. The night was alive with the sound of the woodland creatures with the coo of owls and the rustling of animals in the brush.

"How do you know where you're going?" I asked as we made our way through the trees.

"Gabriel would bring me here often in our earlier years. We'd have picnics, camping, parties, a lot out here. My favorite memory of this place was when he asked me to marry him. He put string lights throughout the trees that led to the clearing. There was an awning covered in flowers, music playing, and lights. It was so beautiful," she remembered.

"Awww, that is so sweet." I could tell he loved her because there were a lot of trees before you got to the clearing. Just the amount of work he put in to make it special for her was admirable.

"Love makes you do more than expected." She unlocked the car door and got in. "That's why you can't stay and wait, isn't it?"

I pressed my lips together and nodded. "Yes."

"When did it start?"

"When we were in Argo," I admitted. I saw how strong of a person he was, his compassion and care. I've been falling ever since.

"I see. Well, I want you to know that I understand. I would do the same if it was Gabriel. I just want you to be safe." She looked over at me and gave a small smile.

"With God, anything is possible," I reminded her. It was something she reminded me of on a regular basis. In fact, it was one of the first scriptures she showed me.

"That's right." She laughed.

Seraph reached over and squeezed me tightly.

"Please be careful." She looked almost as if she wanted to cry. We were sitting in her car up the street from the castle. She drove aways past so I could figure out a way to sneak in. I hugged her back and kissed her cheek. She quickly prayed for me, then swiped a tear from her cheeks. "Call me if you need help." I nodded sharply and climbed out of her car. Even though she drove two blocks past the entrance, we were still at the castle. The gates were ten-feet-high artistically carved metal that gleamed in the sunlight. I held onto a couple bars as I stared at the castle. From where I could see, the castle was surrounded on every angle with guards. I just had to figure out the best way to get past them. Hands in my pockets, I slowly began to walk along the fence away from the two guards who stood at the front entrance. When there it was, a service entrance. I crouched and ran over and climbed inside the door. Managing not to be seen, I kept low as I walked past huge boxes. Hearing a voice, I paused and ducked between two boxes. The voices quickly faded, so I peeked before standing to look around for a door that led inside. I quickly spotted one and ran as quietly as I could to it. I tried to close the door softly, but it made the loudest noise when it shut all the way. The heavy door had to have alerted someone. I was looking around when a guard spotted me.

"Hey you! What are you doing here?" I bolted down the hall-way to the right. I waved my hand and sent boxes flying at the man. They didn't seem too heavy, so I didn't think they would injure him.

One hit him in his left leg as he was running, causing him to fall, but I could hear the static from a walkie-talkie.

"We have an intruder alert. Intruder in the west wing," he spoke as he tried to stand up.

I ran all the way to the end and turned several times before I found another door. I pulled on a massive heavy door. It had a golden lion as the handles and had golden lace along the edge of it. I pulled it open and dropped my mouth. I was in the throne room. I quickly started to back up, but a hand grabbed me and put me in handcuffs. Of all the rooms, I found the throne room. Not only that, but they were in the middle of a sentencing or something! The king and queen sat on their massive throne that shot high up to the high painted ceilings. He was talking when I came in, but now everyone was silent and staring at me as the guard pulled me next to the man and made me sit on my knees on the granite floor. Looking over, I realized that man was Luca.

"What are you doing here?" He hissed under his breath.

"I wanted to help." I clearly was doing a bad job. The plan was to sneak him out not get caught. He sighed and shook his head. The king waved his hand, and the guard left, closing the door behind him. The king then walked up to me and stared.

"You broke into my home," he said simply.

"I was just trying to—" I looked over at Luca. He glanced at him.

"Just what?" He came closer to Luca. "Is this your rescue mission?" he asked, laughing. His deep-throated laugh echoed in the room, reverberating off the walls.

"How noble of you," he snickered. "Now, while I do admire your devotion to this young man here, that does not negate the fact that you broke into my home. Therefore, you will be dealt with accordingly," he told me, no longer laughing.

"Now where was I before I was so rudely interrupted?" He shot me a look. "Ah yes, Luca. You thought you could just come in here and threaten me? Why, I've done nothing wrong!" He was pacing slowly back and forth in front of us.

"You're a liar! You murdered those people in Argo!" he yelled, pulling against his restraints.

"*I* did not murder those people. My men did. Besides, all I do is give a job, and they carry it out how they see fit. Really, I had no *idea.*" The king's voice was low but not in a deep way. It was like the growl of a lion when it's hunting.

"Your men, your crime. They only do what you tell them."

"Yes, they are loyal, aren't they? Regardless of who ordered what, you came here, to me. Why?"

"To kill you, of course."

He laughed out loud. "Oh my boy, you are so funny." He walked up close and grabbed his face in his hand. "Did you really think you could come here and kill me and it would be that easy? If you want to kill me, you're going to have to work for it," he jeered.

"I plan to," Luca seethed.

The king smiled, wagging his finger at Luca. "You were always my favorite. Baku was weak."

"Don't you dare talk about Baku." Luca spit.

"Shame what happened to him. If he was strong like you, maybe he would have survived."

"What did you do?"

"*I* didn't do anything. He got in the way." Luca looked down at the floor, his eyes wide, his veins in his temples bulging.

"Jasper!" the queen called from her chair. He looked over at her as she stood up. She strutted over in her elegant gown. She stood behind him, staring at us with lowered catlike eyes. Her long red nails peeked through the sleeves of her bright-blue gown as she lifted her hands and placed them on his broad shoulders. Her thick lips grazed his ear as she whispered into it while her other hand stroked his arm. He was dressed in a similar fashion that was draped over his tall muscular body like it was made specifically for him. He smiled sinisterly as she pulled away from him. She briefly looked into his eyes and touched his face. Her fingertips glided through his beard as she sauntered to her throne beside his. Her robe flew behind her as she walked until she pulled on it as she turned. Eyes locked on mine, she sat and crossed her legs as her long nails tapped the marble chair impatiently. The king ran a hand over his beard where she touched him and turned to face us.

"My wife thinks I should kill you both," he told us matter-of-factly. My body ran hot with nervousness as I looked over at her. She was still staring at us under her full eyelashes. I looked back at the king. I felt Luca stiffen beside me.

"However," he said as he slowly walked down the marble steps toward us, "I don't want to do that." He stopped directly in front of me. "I like you." Luca growled and pulled against his restraints. The king glanced at him, smirking. "You stay, and I'll let your friend go."

"Don't do it, Ora."

"Jasper," the queen barked from her chair. He turned to face her. "We already have an omnikinetic and don't need another." She snapped her fingers. Immediately a guard dragged a woman in by her shackles. She was sweating profusely, her long curly hair sticking to her face. There was a tie around her mouth, preventing her from speaking. She wore a lavender peasant dress and no shoes. Her face was smudged, but from where I stood, I could tell her eyes matched mine. The guard took the tie from her mouth, and she coughed. She brushed her hair out of her face and looked up, locking eyes on me. A single tear dropped from her eyes and onto the floor. The queen looked back and forth between us and stood. She walked over to the woman.

"Do you know this girl?" she asked. The woman quickly looked down at the ground but said nothing. The queen came behind her and grabbed her by her hair and held her head up.

"I asked you a question," she sneered.

"Yes, I know her," she choked out between sobs. My brow furrowed, and I took a step forward. "She's my daughter."

My mouth fell open. *Mom?*

The king's laugh echoed through the room, a harsh sound in the silence. The queen dropped the woman. "Oh how nice. A family reunion." He continued laughing.

"Mom?" I called again, begging her to look at me.

"I knew I liked you. You're just like her. Tell me"—he grabbed one of my locks, his hand sliding down to the end—"are you more powerful than her?" He was inches from my face. I looked over his shoulder at my mom, then lowered my eyes.

"Please leave her alone. I'll do what you wa—" the queen slapped her, making her fall back to the ground. She ran a hand over her hair and flipped it over her shoulder.

"Do be quiet," she told her as the woman cried on the floor.

The king grabbed my face in his hand and stared into my eyes. His were the same color as Luca's. The more I stared, the more similar they became. How could the face of my beloved friend be the same face as this monster? "I think I'll keep you."

"Luca." I saw him lower her head out of the corner of my eye. The king turned and looked at him and waved his hand. A guard immediately untied him.

"You can stay here too, son," he told him as he still held me. My jaw dropped.

"I'd rather die."

The king roughly dropped my face and walked over to him.

"You could be a prince, royalty," he explained as he gestured at everything around him. "Just think of it. All you have to do is join me." He held out his hand to him.

Luca ignored it and walked over to me and pulled me behind his back. "Never."

I couldn't believe King Jasper was his father. This man who killed all of those innocent people was his father. This man who plundered my village. This man who killed nearly their entire village, the one he grew up in! I began to cry for him; I couldn't imagine what he must be feeling right now.

"It'll be okay, Ora," he whispered over his shoulder.

"Please don't lie to the girl. She needs to know the truth. Either you two join me, or you die." King Jasper looked annoyed now like a cat who is growing tired of playing with the mouse. He stepped closer and looked at me over Luca's shoulder.

"Just think, Ora. You could live in this grand palace"—his arms swept around him—"with your mother, who, judging by how long I've had her, hasn't seen you in a while. You'll have everything."

My mother. I looked at her crumpled body on the ground and cried even harder. I just wanted to run into her arms, but I couldn't. Not this way.

"Leave her alone. She wants no part with you," Luca defended.

"And you?" He tilted his head and narrowed his eyes as he stood in front of Luca.

"You died to me a long time ago," he replied coldly.

"Shame." He turned and walked to his throne chair and sat down. The queen dragged my mother by her chains over to the foot of her chair and sat down.

"Aliza, dear, I'd say goodbye to your daughter if I were you," she sneered. Her head shot up.

"Please, no, I'll do what you want. Don't hurt her." The queen raised her hand.

"Jezebel, I really wish you would decline from abusing the poor woman. What use is she if you give her brain damage?" the king snapped. She rolled her eyes and placed her hand back in her lap.

"Let her talk to her." The guard released Aliza, and she ran over to me and pulled me into a hug. When we pulled back, it was like looking in a mirror. Tears welled in both of our eyes as she looked me over.

"You've gotten so big. And you're so beautiful," she told me in between sobs. I buried my face in her hair and cried as Luca rubbed my back.

"Listen to me, Ora, you need to leave," she whispered into my hair.

"I can't leave you," I choked out.

"I'll be fine, but you can't stay. You must leave now." She pulled away and gave me a firm look. I reluctantly nodded and turned to run but was stopped by a group of guards.

"Ah ah ah," the king mocked in a childlike manner, "and where do you two think you're going?" He called from his chair. "I really wished you'd be more agreeable." He sighed heavily. "Very well, take them to a cell." The guards quickly chained and pushed us toward the door. I turned my head and called for my mother as they dragged me away from her again.

CHAPTER

Luca irritatedly paced the cell as I sat quietly in the corner praying. He huffed and puffed as he muttered to himself. He stopped at the gate and rattled it.

"Luca." He turned and looked at me harshly before his face softened. He sighed and came and sat by me. "Just breathe," I told him. He took a few deep breaths and calmed down.

"I am pissed."

"I know what you mean." I'd only gotten to see my mother for just a moment before she was taken from me.

"He just makes me so angry!" he yelled.

"Did you know he was the one who destroyed Argo?" I asked after a moment. He shook his head and stared at the floor and I waited, but he didn't say anything.

"You knew, didn't you?"

"Someone told me when I was in jail."

"You knew and you didn't tell me" I replied, leaning away from him.

"What was I supposed to say, Ora? Oh hey, by the way, my dad is the one who destroyed Argo. Oh and he's a king too by the way," he snapped.

"You could've told me you at least had a suspicion," I whispered. I was hurt. Argo was my home too. He should have told me.

"Look, I'm sorry, Ora, but it was something I didn't even want to be true. I haven't seen him in years, and I knew he was a terrible guy, but this," he told me waving his hands around, trying to find the words, "this right here is next level." He turned and faced me. "He grew up there, and for him to just have so many people slaughtered like sheep was the most evil thing I've ever seen in my life," he told me, shaking his head.

"The devil must be using him."

"What?"

"Seraph said that people are not all evil. The spirit within them is either evil or good. Those who are evil are being controlled by the devil and the good by God," I replied. He just sat quietly looking at me.

"Ora, I'm sorry," he apologized.

"Luca—"

"No, let me say this, please." He held up his hand, cutting me off. "I shouldn't have said what I said to you, you didn't deserve it. I never wanted to hurt you, but I figured making you mad at me was the only way to keep you safe. If I told you what I knew, I knew you would want to follow me. But that doesn't excuse what I did." He grabbed my hand. "I can't ever say how sorry I really am. I promise I'll get us out of here."

"It's okay, I'm not mad anymore. Although you should have known, I was going to follow you anyways, mad or not." I laughed.

"Yeah, I should've known that, huh?" His thumb brushed back and forth over my knuckles.

"So what's the plan?"

"I'm working on it." He scratched his head.

I stood and walked over to the bars. They were as cold as the ones I was stuck in all of those years. I looked around trying to spot anyone that may be around. Once I noticed we were alone, I lifted the items on the desk up with a quick lift of my hand.

"Luca, come here." He came over and looked back and forth between me and the stuff that was floating over the desk. "Would any of this help?"

"Hmmm." He looked at each item—the stapler, paper clips, paper, pencil. "No, not unless you want to draw some keys to get us out."

"Oh, I have an idea!" I exclaimed, which dropped the items down with a crash. "Oops." I waited a beat to see if anyone would come in, but no one did.

"Can you melt this bar?" He grabbed the bars and squeezed them until they turned red from the heat. I pulled my hands apart to make the bars bend in opposite directions. And *boom*, it was open!

"Awesome. We just need to do this a couple more times and we'll be golden." I smiled with excitement.

Once the opening was big enough, we climbed through to the other side. Luca rustled through the drawers, checking over everything.

"I doubt they left the keys in there."

"Yeah, I just wanted to make sure."

I quietly opened the door and peeked my head around it. No one was around, so I beckoned for Luca to follow.

"Do you know where you're going?" Luca whispered as we ran down the hall on our toes.

"You do remember I lived in a cell most of my life, right? It's pretty much the sa—" I quickly grabbed Luca and pulled him next to me just as two guards started walking down the hall adjacent to us. They opened a door and walked through, and we squatted down.

"If I'm right, the door right there should lead to a hall connected to an outside door."

Just as we rounded the corner, I heard someone whisper my name. I turned to look at Luca but saw my mom behind him standing in front of an open door. I stood upright and ran to her.

"What are you doing?" Luca asked, looking around confused. Once he saw her, he followed behind just as my mom pulled me into the room with her.

She hugged me tightly, her face buried in my hair. She smelled of lavender, and her once sticky hair was now freshly washed and soft as a feather. She pulled away and looked at me crying.

"Alora, my baby." She hugged me again. Her voice was soft and sweet like Esther's was. Tears filled my eyes, and I hugged her back. Over her shoulder, I could see Luca standing there, looking around as he tried to give us some privacy. She eventually let me go and held my hand, leading me to a big blue couch. We sat down, and she smiled as she reached up and stroked my hair.

"I love this," she told me, holding a lock.

The room was tastefully decorated with varying shades of blues, grays, and purples. In the far back of the room was a black canopy bed draped in white curtains. The bed was covered in lavender sheets and plenty of pillows. The more I looked around, the more feminine the room looked—from the vanity by the big windows to the plush carpet.

"Is this your room?" I asked her. Luca came and sat beside me.

She nodded. "Yes, although it's more of a cell. I can't leave it unless summoned."

"It doesn't look too bad of a place to be stuck," Luca noted.

"A prison is still a prison, no matter how beautiful it may look." She snapped. "I've been here since they took me from you." Her eyes pricked with fresh tears.

"He took me from you? Wait, he's the king that started the Separation?" I was shocked remembering Seraph's story.

"He was rounding up Arcadians. When the soldiers arrived, I took you and ran into the jungle. They eventually found us and took you one way and me the other. They were going to kill you, but I told them I would go willingly if they didn't. God must have softened their hearts. At first I thought I'd be able to buy you back from him. But I didn't have any money, and I didn't know where you were."

"She was in a prison outside of Verdea," Luca told her.

She nodded and bit her lip. "I see. Enough about me. Who are you?" she asked Luca, looking around me.

"I'm Luca, ma'am." Her eyes narrowed.

"I see you're a pyro and the king's son."

"He's not like that, Mom." She seemed suspicious of him, and I didn't like it.

"Well, how do you know?" she retorted. "This could all be a plot to capture you too. He could have been sent by his dad to capture you."

"With all due respect, that was the first time I saw my father in over eighteen years. He left my mother when I was a kid."

"Then how did you meet Alora?"

"My godfather was her guard at the prison. He was like a father to both of us. He introduced me to her in hope that I'd open up after my mom passed. Eventually he took a turn for the worse and told me to take care of her," Luca explained.

"He paid off my debt," I added.

"So you're her new guard."

"Mom!"

"What? I'm just curious. He said he told him to take care of you," she defended.

"Let me be clear. I love your daughter. There's nothing I wouldn't do for her. At first, we were just friends, but it's more than that now. So in a way, yes, I am her guard because I would give my life for her. Does that answer your question?" he asked. I turned and looked at him.

"You do?" I asked in disbelief. He tucked a lock behind my ear, smiling.

"I do." My face broke out into a huge grin.

"I apologize. I see you mean nothing but good for her."

"It's okay," he replied, grabbing my hand, holding it in his. "But we really should go before someone notices we're gone."

I looked at my mom. "Come with us."

"You want me to come with you?"

"Yes." She smiled, nodding in agreement. She peeked her head out of the door and motioned for us to follow her.

We walked quietly down the hall when a booming voice stopped us in our tracks.

"Hey!" We turned to see three guards charging toward us.

"Run!" my mom yelled. "I'll hold them off."

"Mom!"

"Ora, we don't have time." Luca pulled my arm as he continued running. I heard glass shatter and men moaning in pain. After a moment, a loud thump and a scream came from my mom. I looked back trying to see what happened.

Luca held my hand and raced to the exit. Eyes blurry with tears, I let him drag me across the lot and onto the street. We raced through traffic, missing cars by seconds as they honked, slamming on the breaks. He ran until we came to a small patch of wood far from the mansion and stopped to catch his breath. I slumped like a doll against a tree and fell to the ground crying. My chest burned as I cried and tried to catch my breath. I felt him kneel in front of me and pull me into his arms.

"We have to go back," I blubbered.

"Ora, you know we can't do that," he advised. I clung to him and cried. He brushed the tears that lingered on my cheeks with a thumb and kissed my forehead. "It'll be okay." I nodded, swiping at my nose, and stood up. He wrapped an arm around my waist and continued deeper into the forest. Eventually, when we came out, we were near Seraph's house.

Seraph opened the door as we walked up the drive. She ran down and met us. Her small figure stretched as she tried to hug us both at once.

"Thank God you're all right." She pulled back smiling, her eyes squinting in the sunlight. "I was so worried." Behind her, Gabriel stood smiling in the doorframe. We walked inside with Seraph in-between us and sat at the kitchen island. Gabriel stood across from us with one arm around Seraph and the other adjusting his circular glasses.

"So what happened?" Seraph prodded, looking between the two of us. Gabriel chuckled and passed us a bottle of water. He exchanged a look with both of us, presumably getting a first-person account of what transpired.

"I found my mom." I looked down at my hands. Luca placed one on top of mine.

"What's the problem? Why do you look sad?"

"After we broke out of the cell, we ran into her. She was coming with us until some guards started coming. She stayed so we could escape," Luca explained, rubbing my back.

"I'm sorry, honey," Seraph sympathized.

"Why was she there?" Gabriel asked after a moment.

"It appears that King Jasper had taken her prisoner and made her do his bidding in his conquests." I hate him even more now," Luca answered.

"He's had her since the Separation," Seraph realized. I rubbed my raw eyes that were most likely swollen like two tomatoes by now.

"Are you two hungry?" she asked, offering us a plate.

I shook my head. "I just want to go to sleep. Excuse me." I stood, pushed in my chair, and headed to the staircase. I walked into our adjoined bathroom and stood in front of the framed mirror. I looked exactly like my mother even though my face was smeared with dirt and oil from bending the bars. My violet eyes were bright against my red sclera but the same shade as hers. I washed my face but then opted for a shower. I pulled my locks into a bun, high on my head, and lay under the covers. I sniffled thinking about all the times I missed with her. All the birthdays, all the years spent behind bars, alone, wondering if she was even alive. It never occurred to me that she was in the same predicament as me. I sighed heavily, pulled the cover over my head, and wept.

A few minutes passed before I felt someone sit near my feet. I balled up tighter under the sheets, my eyes still closed.

"Ora," Luca's deep voice was laced with concern. I sniffled and squeezed my eyes tight. I didn't feel like talking.

"Ora, please talk to me." His warm hand rubbed my back through the duvet. I turned to face him and pulled down the sheets until only my face was showing.

He smiled. "I brought you some food."

"I'm not hungry," I mumbled. He sighed and pulled the cover down more. "Tell me what's wrong." I shook my head. "Ora, tell me what's wrong." I could hear the strain in his voice. I sat up as he placed a hand on the other side of me.

"I should've helped her." I wiped my eyes before any tears could escape. "I should've done something. Now I'll never see her again." I held my face in my hands, feeling terrible. She had been trapped longer than me, and her one chance to escape, she sacrificed to help us.

"You'll see her again," he comforted, rubbing my back.

"How do you know?" I looked into his sunset eyes.

"Because I know you won't let that happen. When you decide what you want to do, please tell me. I don't want you going back there alone, okay?" I nodded and dropped my head on his shoulder. He wrapped me in his arms and kissed me on the forehead.

After a moment, he moved and handed me a plate. "Now eat."

CHAPTER

10

I woke up earlier than the roosters the next morning. Slipping out of bed, I snuck past a sleeping Luca and down the stairs, out the back door. I shivered in the crisp morning air and set off toward the clearing. I was determined to get stronger, to be better. I wanted to save my mother, and I knew I had to do more in order to not be caught this time. I swung my arms as I spun, causing thousands of leaves to swirl above me as if I were a fan. With a graceful curve of my arm, they danced in between the trees and dipped around bushes and flowers. I held my opposite hand up, palm facing the sky and pulled stones and flowers from the ground. I waved my arms as if I was an orchestra conductor and weaved the two in and out of one another. After a moment, I settled them both to the ground and looked around. Some of the tree's foliage was dispersed on the ground from my exercise as the remainder floated down from the sky. I focused my attention on a large boulder not too far from where I stood. I took a deep breath and turned my body to face it. Using one hand, I moved it up, but the boulder didn't budge. I tried again, nothing. I sighed and held out two hands and motioned. The boulder rose two inches off the ground before dropping back down with a loud thump. Frustrated, I yelled and swung my arms up hard and sent the boulder flying into the sky. It came crashing down, breaking into several pieces. I plopped onto my back and stared at the rock fragments. Seraph did express how negative emotions cause negative actions. The rock didn't dance like the leaves did; it rocketed into the air and violently crashed to the earth. *I had to keep myself under control*, I thought to myself. What if someone had been there when it crashed down?

Alora.

I jumped at the voice, looking behind me. No one was there. "It probably was a rabbit or something," I tried to convince myself. No one else is out here, so it must be something else.

Alora.

I stood in place, still as a statue as I scanned my surroundings—just me, the trees, and the morning air. So where was this voice coming from?

"Yes?" I answered, feeling like an idiot for responding.

Your mom is okay, she's safe.

"She is?" I asked, feeling my heart become lighter.

Yes, don't worry. You will see her again. I'll tell you when it's time.

"Thank you," I whispered. Here I was in the woods, alone, talking to the air, and the air responded. And yet I felt a warm fuzzy feeling, like he was good. At a time when I should be terrified about what just happened, I felt safe. I waited for a moment, but he didn't speak again. Starting to think I imagined what just happened, I shook the thoughts from my head, dusted off my butt, and started on my morning run.

*****

I walked into the house a sweaty mess. My stomach growled as I followed my nose to the kitchen. I slid into a chair beside Luca as Seraph placed a plate of food in front me. The steam rolled off her world-famous omelets, making my mouth water. I said a quick prayer and dove right in.

"You were up early today," Gabriel noted, smirking.

"I wanted to get some training in," I replied, shoveling food into my eagerly waiting mouth.

Seraph smirked at my almost empty plate and dropped another dab of butter into the sizzling pan.

"Slow down before you choke." Luca snickered as he wiped his mouth. I stuck my tongue out and spooned the last bit into my mouth.

"Seraph, your food is always delicious. Can I stay here forever?"

"As long as you want, honey." She smiled, handing me a bowl of fruit. I finished my food gratefully and kissed Seraph's cheek, making my way upstairs for a shower.

Once I was dressed, I bounced down the stairs to meet Luca by the door. I was in a good mood, and I couldn't wait to share with him what happened out in the field. He would either be able to tell me what happened or think I was insane. I figured it would be the latter. We walked into the backyard and through the rose garden. He didn't speak at first, so I decided now or never.

"Luca, I have a question."

"Ask away."

"Okay, so let's say someone is alone and they hear a voice calling them—" I started. He shot a look up at me and smirked.

"Uh-huh."

"So said person realizes no one is around, so it wasn't some-one they knew. Would you answer?" I continued searching his eyes, which only reflected his amusement.

"The real question is, did you respond?" He chuckled at my look of surprise. Of course, he would figure out it was me; I don't even know what the whole scenario was for.

"Yes." We sat down on the bench. "He told me my mom was okay and that he'd tell me when to go see her again." He listened intently with his head tilted slightly in the palm of his hand.

"Well, that's comforting. Did he seem bad or something?"

"That's the thing, I didn't feel scared. It felt like I was talking to you," I told him, trying to understand it myself.

"Well, next time he says something, ask him who he is," he sug-gested. I definitely would the next time we talked. We finished our walk in the garden chatting about various things. It wasn't until our fingers started to get numb that we decided to go inside for something hot to drink. Tea for me and coffee for him. We sat in the sitting room and sipped our beverages as we read our individual books. I watched Luca from my seat, thinking about how lucky I was to have him as a friend. He sat reclined in a chair, holding his book, *Don Quixote*, over his face. His feet were crossed at the ankles, one foot jiggling. I smiled when he peeked over his book at me with narrowed eyes.

"What?"

"I love you too," I confessed. His face broke in a huge smile as he looked back at his book.

"I knew it," he gloated. I laughed and went back to my novel.

*****

A few days later, I had a nagging feeling. The voice hadn't spoken to me, but I felt like I should go. It felt like I was being pushed to go. I'd ignored it, trying to busy myself with helping Seraph at the library. I stood awkwardly in front of the desk as she stacked books onto a cart by section. She briefly looked up at me for a second, her glasses falling slightly down her nose.

"What was that story we read last night?" I asked, fiddling with the pamphlets that sat in the metal container.

"Ah, it was about Moses. We were in Exodus. Do you have any questions about it?" she asked, still filling.

"Do you think it is possible for him to have turned away from God? I mean to not do what he wanted him to do?"

"Well, of course, it is possible. We all are given a choice, but think of what would have happened if he did. All of his people would have been stuck in Egypt," she expressed as she finished. "The task may seem daunting, but God will only ask you to do something he knows you are capable of. When he speaks, you should consider it an honor because he chose you to do something for him." She smiled, leaning forward on her elbows.

"What if you're scared?" I was still messing with the objects on her desk, messing their neat little piles.

"Fear is a natural reaction, but you cannot let it control you. You need to make your faith stronger than your fear. God will not bring you to the mountain and just leave you there. If he brought you to it, he will bring you through it," she replied knowingly. I pressed my lips together, nodding my head. I understood what she meant. And truthfully, I was honored that he would pick me to do something for him. I knew that something was to go back to confront King Jasper and save my mom. I just didn't know how I'd go about it just yet.

Shoulders back I walked straight up to the gate. I was not going to sneak in this time. The guard held up a hand to me, stopping me in my tracks.

"State your business," the guard demanded as he stood towering over me like a building.

"I want to see King Jasper," I said to his chest. He barked out a laugh before grabbing his walkie-talkie.

"We've got an Arcadian here to see King Jasper," he relayed over the radio. A static voice came over saying to let me in. The other guard that stood beside the giant escorted me inside. We walked down the hall Luca and I escaped from just a few weeks ago, my eyes lingering on my mother's bedroom door. He knocked at the throne room, and someone opened the large doors and let us in. The guard walked me to the center, then walked back out the door.

"Well, well, well, if it isn't the little escape artist." King Jasper sat on his throne, legs crossed. His clothing was red and made of silk, much like the first one I'd seen him in. His wife sat beside him wrapped in lavender. Her long legs were crossed in front of her as she sat and stared at me with her cat eyes. He stood and came toward me with a broad smile on his lips. He walked slowly around me in wide circles, his red robe flowing gently behind him.

"You came back."

"Of course," I told him firmly. I wouldn't let him intimidate me. I wouldn't let him get to me.

"You've come to accept my offer then."

"I've come for my mother." He stopped, making circles and looked at me with a sly smile.

"Interesting. First you escaped, causing me to *reevaluate* my guards"—he smiled wickedly—"now you come back making demands? What makes you think I will comply?"

I started to say something, but he snapped his fingers, and the guards brought my mother out. He walked behind her, untying her restraints. She stood up cautiously, rubbing her wrists. He motioned toward me, and she ran over and hugged me.

"I do love a good family reunion. Now"—he walked toward his throne and turned in front of it—"you can be with her under one condition. Stay here," he added, smiling wickedly.

Don't do it, Alora. My eyes widened. He finally came back to talk to me. *It's a trap.*

"I know," I said out loud. My mom looked at me with a furrowed brow.

"Who are you talking to?" she inquired, confused. I ignored her and waited for the voice to speak again. Just silence.

"No, we're both going," I replied defiantly to the king. "You're going to let both of us go."

His deep throat laugh vibrated through the walls and echoed off the high ceilings. He laughed so hard he almost fell out of his chair.

"Let me be clear," his accent thickening, "I'm not letting you both leave. You both stay, or one of you dies," he clarified.

"What, you can't do that!"

"I should be doing more when you destroyed my property, trespassed, and then had the *audacity*," his voice rose, "to come back making demands! It would serve you well to keep your thoughts to yourself. Especially when I'm the one holding your life in balance," he sneered, his eyes darting back to mine. He came close, his fiery eyes radiating heat, and twisted a lock in his hand.

"Now, what is your answer?"

Tell him no, the voice said loudly in my ear.

"No," I whispered, shaking.

"Speak up," he barked.

Tell him louder!

"No!" I yelled. My face stung from the sudden slap that crossed my face. Stars danced in my line of vision as my head swam. I fell to the floor in a heap.

My mother's scream pierced the room as he grabbed her by the roots of her hair.

"Both of you women insist on making me the bad guy!" he scolded. "Well, you've made your choice clear!" He yanked a sword from a guard's belt and held it at her throat.

I struggled to stand up, my legs shaking.

Don't worry, I'll be with you.

I screamed, causing the sword to fly from his arm and into the wall behind me. I swung my arms and sent all of the weapons in the room flying into the ceiling, causing the chandelier to shatter into a million pieces. Jasper shot my mother away from him as he darted away from the falling glass. Furious, he dropped his robe from his shoulders and, with one slick motion, shot a ball of fire at me, which I luckily dodged. The queen stood up and sashayed her way out of the room.

"Leave her alone!" my mother yelled from the ground, blood dripping down her forehead.

"You insolent woman!" He shot flaming rings at me that I diffused with a swipe of wind. The guards backed up against the wall, giving us space. My mother looked on in horror.

"You're a fool for thinking I'd just let you both walk out of here!" He blew a fire in a rush toward me. I ripped a curtain from the walls and let it catch fire. With a quick twist of my arms, I rang it and whipped it toward him. He yelped as the tip swung back and singed his bare shoulder.

"Agh!" He pumped his fists in rapid motions sending balls of fire shooting at me as I ran trying to avoid being hit. The more he missed, the angrier he became. The flames hit various pieces of furniture, setting them each ablaze, heating up the room. King Jasper stopped, breathing heavily as he stalked me like a panther. Guards behind him scattered around frantically, trying to get away from the growing flames.

"You are powerful. I will admit that." His broad chest heaved with a sinister smile. "You would make a wonderful asset to my collection." He reached out, and a giant flaming hand reached out and grabbed my mother. She screamed as the flames licked her body.

Pull your arm back

I pulled my arm back like I was drawing a bow and released it. The remaining fragments of a table flew from behind me and into King Jasper. The embers hit his eyes, causing him to drop my mother. I lifted her from the ground gently and put her in the hallway and closed the door, locking it behind her. She banged on the door and twisted the knob, trying to get in. His screams of pain radiated through the room as he batted his eyes trying to get the cinders out. I lifted him up high into the air and shot him into his throne. I twisted my wrists and tied curtains and vines from the plants around him so he couldn't get out. I swung a single hand behind me as I walked toward him putting out the fires. I climbed the stairs and stood directly in front of him. His eyes were bloodshot red from irritation against his orange eyes. He squirmed in his seat as he shot deadly glares at me.

"Release me!" he demanded.

"Why did you destroy Argo?" I inquired as I paced back and forth in front of him.

"They had something that I wanted, so I took it. It is as simple as that!" He tried to set the binds on fire, but there was no way he could without burning himself in the process.

"You cannot just take things! You've murdered so many innocent people. How could you be this heartless?" I was trying to figure him out. I was trying to understand.

"Because I wanted to!" He screeched as he set the binds on fire, burning his arms and part of his chest. The binds melted off, and he bolted out of the chair and tackled me.

We rolled down the steps and onto the marble floor. His fists connected with my torso as I rolled trying to throw him off me. I heaved in pain as he stood up. His foot connected to my stomach repeatedly as I screamed in agonizing pain. I begged God to help me as I lay in the fetal position trying to protect myself. The doors burst open into flames behind him, and there stood Luca.

"Get off her!" The king looked over at him and stepped on my leg.

"Aggghh!" I yelled, the pain climbing up my body. Luca rushed forward. Jasper pressed down harder. Luca tackled him to the ground.

"Luca! Luca, stop!" He stopped, his fist hovering over his father. He pushed him away and rushed over to me.

"Are you okay? Is it broken?" He looked me over frantically.

"I'd say so." His face broke.

"Oh Ora, I'm so sorry. I should have come quicker," he apologized.

"It's not your fault. I ran off without telling anyone. I should've told you what I was going to do like you asked."

"I'm so glad you're okay." He kissed my forehead and held his to mine. He stood up and held out a hand. He turned, and I looked to see what he was staring at, and that's when I noticed it. The king was gone.

"He's getting away!" Luca exclaimed, starting to go after him.

"Luca." He looked down at me on the floor and helped me up. I wobbled as I balanced on one foot while holding up my broken leg.

"He got away," he repeated, looking flustered. I smiled, which earned me a look you only reserve for crazy people.

"It's okay."

"No, it's not! He needs to go to—"

"It's okay, God will deal with him," I told him simply. After the encounter I just had with him, I was absolutely positive that he would.

He released a heavy sigh and scooped me up in his arms. He carried me out of the throne room, which was now reduced to scarce walls and large piles of ash and debris. On the other side of the door, I expected to see my mom, but she was gone too.

"Mom? Mom!" I called down the hall. When she didn't answer, Luca carried me to her room, but she wasn't in there either. We walked outside and into the night, and in my heart, I knew he'd taken her.

It'll be okay, the voice told me, and I believed that it would be.

*****

Seraph clung to me crying as Gabriel examined my leg. He squatted beside me, his old knees creaking with the motion. He adjusted his spectacles and looked up at me.

"It is definitely broken," he said apologetically. "Let me go get my medic bag." He slowly stood and jogged to the house.

Luca had carried me all the way back to the house on his back. Seraph and Gabriel ran out as soon as they saw us. I was now sitting on a porch swing with my leg propped up on the table for Gabriel to examine. Turns out he used to be a doctor before he retired and bought the store.

"All right," he said, placing his bag on the ground. "this part is going to hurt."

I screamed in pain as he moved the bone back in place. He wrapped it up with a splint and bandages and sat it gently back on the pillow. "Don't put any pressure on this for six weeks," he instructed. I nodded and accepted the ice Seraph handed me.

"How will I get around?" I had never broken anything before. I didn't know how to walk without putting pressure on it.

"I can carry you," Luca offered. I smiled and turned back to Gabriel. It was nice for him to offer, but it would become a burden sooner or later.

"I'd suggest crutches until you can get a boot that will allow you to put some pressure on it. Six weeks most likely." He placed his things back in his bag and patted my hand.

Six weeks? I sighed heavily as I looked at my broken ankle.

"It will be all right, let's look at the bright side. It could have been much worse." Seraph smiled as she hugged my shoulders.

"Yeah, especially since you approached the king on your own."

Seraph nodded. "Yes, I heard you fought bravely, I am most proud."

"So brave in fact that she sent the king running off like a scared animal," Luca bragged laughing.

"I had help," I said with my head up looking at the sky.

Seraph looked up at the sky trying to see what I was looking at. "She hears voices, you know."

"Not just any voice." She smiled knowingly. "It was God, wasn't it?"

I smiled, still looking at the sky. This time, I was 100 percent sure who that voice was.

CHAPTER

A few weeks later, I sat at the island, my leg on the stool beside me and watched as Luca packed our things into the car. We were heading back to Argo. It took awhile for him to collect all of my belongings that I had accumulated from everywhere we went. Not to mention the mountain of clothing Seraph had bought for me during our time here. It seemed like every other day, there was something new sitting in a nicely wrapped box on my bed. I'll admit it was nice having more than two outfits to choose from. Luca, who was bearing the brunt of the work, did not seem to mind as he stacked our things into the back of Esther's car.

"Are you sure you can't stay?" Gabriel asked, his gray eyes sparkling.

"I wish I could, but Luca is the kiongozi. They need him, and we've already been gone a long time." I did not want to leave them either. I'd grown to love them both dearly. But we had been gone a long time; it was just spring when we left, and now it seemed like it was right around the corner.

"Well, let him go and you stay. He's the moodier one anyways," Gabriel joked with a mischievous grin.

"I heard you," Luca called as he walked down the hall with another bag. Seraph hit him in his arm, then hugged me. He held his arm, rubbing it as if her light punch hurt.

"Leave the girl alone, Gabriel. She's a woman who needs to live her life," she said, her voice cracking.

"Aw, Seraph, please don't cry," I told her as tears rose in my eyes.

"I'm not." She waved her hand while using the other to pinch the top of her nose. "Okay, I am," she confessed after a moment. "It's just that you are like a daughter to me, and I just hate to see you go."

"To both of us," Gabriel added with a hand on her shoulder as tears fell from his eyes.

I hugged them both tightly as we all stood there crying. "I love you guys too," I told them, kissing each of their cheeks. Heat dispersed as we separated, everyone wiping their faces. "I will be back to visit, I promise." They bobbed their heads, too choked up to respond. I adjusted my boot, took each of their hands, and walked to the door.

Luca closed the trunk just as we stepped on the porch. He picked me up and carried me down the numerous steps and placed me at the foot of the staircase. Seraph and Gabriel followed behind, hand in hand.

"Behave yourself, young man. Take care of our sweet girl." Gabriel hugged Luca, clapping his back.

"I will."

"And make sure you guys come back and visit," Seraph told him with a kiss on his cheek.

"We will." He thanked them both for everything and, after another round of hugs, went to start the car. I stood across from them both, holding their hands. We all smiled sadly and pulled in for another group hug.

"Always remember to let God lead you in all you do," Seraph reminded me as she cupped my cheek in her hand. I gave them each another hug and kiss before I hobbled to the car. I stuck my head out of the open window as I waved goodbye to them until they disappeared from sight.

The scenery was breathtaking. I watched skyscrapers turn into tall trees and valleys. The sun shone just over the rolling hills as we neared Argo. It only took us a few hours to get there, but I was already starting to get sleepy. My eyelids became heavy as my head slowly dropped onto the window.

"Ora, wake up. We're here." Luca nudged me awake. I looked around in the darkness and found his glowing eyes in his seat.

"*Hmm?*" I mumbled, my head falling back on the window. I groaned in protest as he shook my shoulders.

"Come on, Ora, wake up." He laughed. I shook my head, keeping my eyes closed. I heard the door open and shut. Cold wind blew in as he opened my door, scooping me in his arms. My boot hit the door, making me let out a little yelp.

"I'm sorry," he apologized, closing the door with his foot. He carried me inside his house and laid me on the bed. The house was warm and smelled like cinnamon. I felt him pull off my shoes and pull the covers up over me. He kissed me on the forehead and closed the door behind me. I pulled the covers up over my shoulders and drifted back to sleep.

*****

I yawned, stretching my sore muscles. Sitting in a car for hours at a time would make your bones so stiff. I walked into the living room and saw a drooling Luca sprawled out on the couch. I giggled as a loud snore made his big chest rise and fall. I walked back into the hall and looked around trying to find a towel and washcloth so I could take a shower. The air-conditioner in the car died about halfway through the ride, so I was pretty sticky. I found one in a closet at the end of the hall. It was organized and filled with towels, sheets, and toiletries. I grabbed a blue towel and went into the bathroom to my right. It was red and white with a nice walk-in shower and double vanity. A potted plant sat in the corner across from the toilet. I turned on the hot water and climbed in, letting the heat melt away my stickiness. I put my clothes on in the bathroom in case Luca woke up. It was a nice lavender dress with wavy sleeves that went to my elbow. The bottom swirled in a circle when I spun, and to make it better, it had pockets. Pockets! Needless to say, it was becoming my favorite article of clothing. I pulled my hair into a ponytail and left the bathroom door open to let out the steam. After putting my towel in the hamper, I washed my hands and took a deep breath as I walked toward the kitchen.

"It's just eggs, you got this," I mumbled to myself trying to give myself a pep talk. I peered into the kitchen and got the necessary ingredients. "*Hmm*, do I want to be fancy and put vegetables in it?" I asked myself. "Yup."

I pulled out eggs, milk, butter, spinach, cheese, and peppers. I quietly set the pan on the stove and turned it on. Dropping butter in the pan, I hummed to myself as I cut up the vegetables. I popped them in the pan and repeatedly ate a piece every so often until it tasted soft. Hey, you can never be too sure. I put the egg mixture in, sprinkled it with seasoning salt, and stirred until it became solid and dropped the cheese in. Once it melted to my satisfaction, I turned off the stove and put the eggs on two plates. Grabbing some forks, I headed to the living room and saw Luca sitting up, smiling.

"Good morning," I said.

"Good morning." He looked down smirking. "So that's what you were doing?"

My eyes lowered. "Why are you smiling like that?"

"You know talking to yourself is the first sign of insanity," he told me, holding back a laugh.

"You heard me? How long were you awake?" I was so embarrassed. I had a bad habit of talking to myself, but no one had ever heard me.

"Long enough to hear you give yourself a pep talk." He grabbed his plate and took a mouthful.

"I, uh..." I was so embarrassed I couldn't even look at him. I sat in the chair across from him and quietly ate my eggs. I looked at him after my second bite, my eyes widening. He was already done.

"Now that was good," he complimented. I thanked him and grabbed his plate after finishing my own to put our dishes in the sink.

I sat on the couch reading my Bible while he took a shower. He practically bounced over to me, smiling like always. He'd been happier ever since we left the castle. Perhaps he finally got everything off his chest to his father. He was dressed in autumn colors that made his eyes shine. His short sleeves revealed the many tattoos I'd admired when we first met, each one a delicate and intricate design. I unconsciously touched my own that I had and smiled.

Walking out of the house, we decided the first person we wanted to see was Esther. She practically tackled us before we could get in the door.

"Habari watoto wangu [Hello my children]!" she greeted in her native tongue.

"Shikamoo mama [Hello, mother]." Her face swelled with pride when she heard me pronounce the phrase correctly. She pulled us into a bear hug, her big arms just shy of encircling us.

"When did you get back?" she asked, ushering us into her house.

"Late last night," Luca replied, sitting on a pillow. "Ora slept at my house. We didn't want to wake you."

"Natumahi ulijiendesha [I hope you behaved yourself]," she scolded.

"Of course." I giggled from my seat at Luca's surprised face.

"Watu wawili hawapaswi kuwa katika nyumba moja ikiwa hawajaoa," she continued eyeing him.

"Bado hatujaolewa," he replied, smiling at me. I looked between them and narrowed my eyes. A smile broke out on her face.

"What are you two talking about?" I asked suspiciously.

"Nothing, darling. I'm just messing with him. Now we must go tell everyone you are back. I know they are all anxious to see you."

"What happened since we were gone?" He stood and helped me up.

"A lot actually. I'd say if you want to change your mind about being the kiongozi, I think I'd be a master at it," she joked, elbowing him.

Esther was right. As we walked around the village, I was impressed by the progress that was made since we left. Not only were all of the homes rebuilt, but each was unique and more modern than before. The once dirt paths were now streets made of stone that led to each business and home. Flowers and trees were strategically placed around the town along with benches and trash cans. The statue gleamed from its new paint job. The once mossy dragon was now clean and a bright red with green eyes. It looked so realistic I had to stop for a moment.

"Who painted this?" Luca asked as he inspected it.

"I did," a woman's voice replied behind the statue. Adara smiled as she stepped in front of us.

"Adara!" I screamed as I rushed over to give her a hug.

"Oh my gosh, Ora! I missed you so much." She hugged me back. "When did you get back?"

"Last night."

"Awesome. But yeah, I did this as a favor to Esther. She practically harassed me until I said yes."

"You are a talented artist. Shame you don't use your gift," Esther pointed out.

"This is incredible," Luca complimented.

The closer I looked, the more I was amazed. Every single scale was a slightly different shade of the scale beside it. You could see every last detail, even down to the reflection in its eyes.

Adara decided to show me around as Luca and Esther attended a meeting. The town was completely transformed, and I was so happy to see everyone. Once the tour concluded, we sat down at a bench near a fountain surrounded by flowers. There was something I wanted to discuss with her.

"So how are you doing?" Her husband died during the attack, and I'd felt so bad for leaving soon after.

"I'm doing okay. Some days are better than others," she told me quietly as she drew in on herself.

"How are the kids?" I could only imagine how those kids were handling it.

"Enoch isn't taking it too well. He hasn't been back to school since it happened. The other boys are too young to really know what's going on. I just wish there was more I could do for them," she confessed. "I feel so helpless."

I empathized with her as I hugged her. To lose someone that close to you must be immensely painful. My mother and I may have been apart, but I at least knew that wherever she was, she was still alive. But death is finite. There are no second chances when death came. There wasn't another opportunity to tell people how you feel. To see them. Even though we were not married, Luca was the closest person to me. It hurt to even think about losing him.

"Would you pray with me?" she asked.

"Of course."

We prayed together on the bench. I asked God to comfort her and her children, to give her strength, to give her guidance. I asked Him to show her what to do in this new stage of life, for direction. As we closed the prayer, I could feel her spirit lighten.

"Thank you," she cried, hugging my neck.

"Anytime."

*****

Adara eventually had to go pick up the kids, so we parted ways. Since Luca was still busy, I decided to talk a walk by myself. I wandered down the path we took my first day here and up toward the cave. I wandered inside hoping to find Umilele. The cave wasn't as dark as before due to the sun being higher in the sky. Sadly, she wasn't there. I made my way back to the entrance and stopped in my tracks. Someone stood at the opening, but with the light shining behind them, I couldn't tell who it was.

"Hello?" I called. They didn't answer. They stood there motionless like a statue. I took a deep breath and kept my guard up as I walked in their direction. I had to get past. The closer I got, the more my brow furrowed. It was a man; he was strangely tall and looked familiar.

"Excuse me," I said, trying to get around him as he blocked the entrance. He was a good foot taller than me, so he had to bend his head down to look at me. His face was covered with stubble that was peppered with grays. Gray hairs shined in his curly hair, but he still looked young in the face.

"What?" he said, sounding confused. His deep voice even sounded familiar.

"I said excuse me. I'm trying to get by," I told him. He looked at me as if he was trying to figure out why I was talking to him. Then it struck me; he was the man I saw in the library that day. But what was he doing here? I wondered. His eyes said he was from here, but I hadn't seen him here before. He went around me and headed into the cave. I watched as he walked slowly in, tired almost.

"Hey!" I called. He stopped and slowly turned his head. "Do you live in here?"

"Why?" he retorted, looking annoyed.

"I was just wondering…," my voice drifted.

"They don't want me down there." He turned his head back and walked inside, disappearing into the deep darkness.

I made my way back down the mountain and into the town, wondering who that man was and why no one wanted him here.

"Ora!" Luca yelled from across a field. I hobbled over to him and Esther, who was busy putting her hair up.

"Hey, where did you go?" he asked with a worried look. "We saw Adara, but she said she left you awhile ago."

"Yeah, I was just…," I stopped looking up at where I just came from. "Did you know there's a man living up there?"

His forehead creased. "Up where?"

"In Umilele's cave. He was there when I was coming out," I told him.

His brow creased deeper. "He was in the cave with you? Are you okay? He didn't hurt you, did he?" he questioned as he looked me over.

"No, I'm fine." I shook my head. "He said no one would want him down here."

"What did he look like?" Esther asked, speaking for the first time.

"He had eyes like yours, curly hair, and a wide nose and lips. Oh, and he had a scar over his right eye," I recounted. Her eyes widened.

"Akarudi [He returned]," she whispered.

"Who?" Luca and I asked in unison.

"My son Ade." She looked between us. "Show me where he is."

Luca protested at first, arguing that we should just leave him be, especially after what happened here and how it would stir up old wounds, but he eventually agreed. Making our way up the mountain, we stopped at the entrance as Esther went in, holding a lamp.

We heard low voices coming from inside as we waited.

"Are you going to let him stay in the village?" I asked Luca.

"Only if he apologizes to everyone and works to repay what he helped destroy," Luca declared.

"Yeah, that sounds like a good idea." I agreed. He had to say something to those he hurt, people like Adara.

"God wants us to show others mercy, and I'm trying to do that. However, his actions have repercussions. We cannot just let him come back like nothing happened. No, he has to earn back trust. Although with some people, that may be impossible," he thought out loud as Esther and Ade walked out.

"Luca," he said as he recognized him.

"Ade."

"This is Ora," Esther introduced. He stared at me for a moment until Luca shifted uncomfortably beside me.

"Hi, Ade." I gave him a small smile.

"Hello, Ora," his deep voice murmured. He dragged his eyes from me and looked at his mom.

"He wants to come back with us," Esther announced, looking at Luca. She knew it was really his call.

"If you do," he turned his attention to Ade, "you need to apologize to the village. You've caused a lot of pain." Ade nodded in agreement. "You will volunteer around the village to help rebuild what you helped destroy. We can forgive you, but it's up to you to get right with God," Luca added.

"That's fine. You have my word." He ran a hand through his hair, glancing at me.

Luca nodded once, grabbed my hand, and helped me down the mountain. I heard Ade chuckle behind me as we walked away. They followed close behind as we all headed back to the village. I sat on a bench in the meeting circle. Luca stepped on the stage and sounded the horn that signaled a meeting. People left their individual homes and gathered in the circle. Esther and Ade stood off to the side of the stage as they waited for everyone to arrive.

"Good evening, everyone, I am so glad to see all of you. During my time apart, I have found out what I sought after, and now with a clear mind, I hope we can all move on to a brighter future." Everyone clapped and cheered. He waited until they were done to continue, "That being said, there is someone who would like to speak with you all." Luca motioned to Ade and stepped aside. Ade stepped up and faced the crowd.

"Some of you may remember me, some of you may not. My name is Ade Gbeho, son of Esther Gbeho." A low murmur erupted in the crowd. "I have wronged you all. I lost my way and joined those who desired only to bring you harm. I betrayed you all, something that is unforgivable. Samhani Sana [Very sorry]. I know the pain I caused you all is real and something that will not go away. But I will work to prove how sorry I am. I just hope you can find it in your heart to forgive me. Thank you." He stepped down from the stage and went back by his mother. The crowd was still talking amongst themselves. From the sound of it, some were upset, some were angry, and some people thought they should give him a chance. I looked at Luca and stood on top of my bench above the crowd.

"I think we should give him a chance," I said out loud. The crowd hushed as everyone turned to face me.

"He helped the people who murdered my family!" someone yelled. The crowd agreed.

"I know he helped hurt all of us in some way. But he at least deserves forgiveness. All of us have done wrong at some point in our lives and needed the forgiveness of others. Forgive as your father in heaven forgives you," I stressed to the crowd. After a bit of debate, they seemed to agree. Luca walked back on the stage.

"Ora is right. We must give Ade a second chance to prove himself to us. He has agreed to volunteer his time to help throughout the village. Let him prove himself before you pass judgment." After a little debate amongst the people, everyone agreed to give him a chance. Luca dismissed, and conversations broke out as everyone walked home in pairs or groups.

The sun was now setting, so we all headed to Esther's house for dinner. She sat everything on the table in front of us before sitting at its helm. We said grace and dug in.

"Thank you for what you said," Ade said before eating his food.

I put a hand over my mouth to hide the food in it. "It's no problem. I just felt they needed some encouragement to give you another chance. Everyone deserves forgiveness."

"Not everyone would think so, so thank you." He smiled, picking up his fork.

"You would make a lovely kiongozi, Ora. You remind me a lot of his mother, Kya. Maybe Luca will let you have his job," Esther joked.

"Don't you have to be from here though?"

"Honey, all of us have already adopted you as our own," she made known. I smiled. I always wanted somewhere to belong, and now I did.

"Thanks, but Luca is the real natural. You sounded like a true leader up there," I bragged, looking into his sunset eyes. He smiled and continued eating his food.

"Where are you from?" Ade asked.

"Originally Arcadia, but I did not grow up there. I spent a lot of time outside, Verdea." I glanced at Luca. "This has been my only real home." Esther reached over and squeezed my hand.

"I've meant to ask you," I said, changing the subject, "how old are you?"

"I am thirty-three," he replied, taking a sip of his water. My eyebrows shot up. I was way off. His face made me think he wasn't too much older than me, but then again, I guessed he was nearing fifty by his hair. "You must be in your early twenties."

"I'm twenty-two" I confirmed.

"Hmmph," he grunted, going back to his food.

"If you don't mind me asking, what made you join King Jasper?" He looked at me over the rim of his cup as he drank his water before answering.

"It's a long story." I looked at him, waiting. He sighed then continued, "A long time ago, I was young and in love. Addah was the most beautiful girl I'd ever seen. The most amazing woman. One day she got very sick and eventually died. I was needless to say, torn up about it. I wasn't my best during that time. I was angry with the world and often got into trouble. When Jasper came around, it gave me something to do, something to take my mind off what had happened. So I joined."

"You were lost," I thought out loud. It made everything make sense. Perhaps when he was destroying the village, he thought he could burn her from his memory so it didn't hurt so much. Hearing his story made me feel kind of bad for him.

"Yes. But now that I'm older and more time has passed, I realize where I went wrong, my mistakes and shortcomings." He turned to face his mom. "I'm really sorry, Mom."

Smiling, she patted his hand. "Ni sawa mwanangu [It's okay, son]," she told him, returning to her food. Light conversation floated as we finished our dinner. We gathered in the living area, each of us sitting on the floor on one of Esther's oversized pillows.

"I think you can start with the remainder of the construction. There are still some things we have to get done," Luca announced to Ade.

He nodded slowly. Eventually it was time for Luca to leave, but he loitered by the door.

"Ora, can I speak with you for minute?" he asked. I followed him outside and to the side of Esther's new porch.

"What's up?"

"I think you should come back with me."

"To where?"

"My house." I looked at him, confused, then it struck me.

"Is this about Ade?"

He walked around me, and I turned to face him. "I'm just not comfortable leaving you here," he told me, searching my eyes.

I knew Luca; he was protective to the core and didn't do things without a valid reason, so I didn't protest. We went back inside and told Esther the new sleeping arrangement.

"That would probably be best," she reaffirmed, glancing at the bathroom where Ade was. "Besides I just have the two beds."

"So it's settled." Luca grabbed my toiletries.

"Good night."

"Good night."

We walked back to his house in the dark with only the sound of crickets chirping and our sneakers on the stone path. Once inside, the familiar scent of cinnamon relaxed me and instantly made me sleepy. Luca made up the bed for me and handed me my toiletries, closing the door behind him.

I changed into my pajamas, a set of flannel pants and shirt. I slipped on a pair of socks and dragged the blanket around me as I walked out to the living room. Luca scooted over on the couch, making room for me. I faced him with my feet in front of me.

"Are you sleepy?" he asked. I nodded, rubbing my eyes. "Go to bed then, it's late."

"Wait, I wanted to talk to you." I yawned.

"What's up?"

"What's the deal with you and Ade?" I questioned. I'd sensed the tension at the dinner table and earlier at the mountain.

He glanced at me briefly. "There's no deal."

"Come on, you were eyeing him and even trying to restrain yourself at times from saying something. I could see it all over your face," I pressed. He was dodging the question.

"He doesn't have the best track record for treating people with respect, especially women. I think Adah was the only woman he ever did treat with respect," Luca said. "Besides, I didn't like the way he was looking at you."

"He only looked at me because I was talking," I pointed out.

He shook his head. "No one should look at you like that. That is reserved for only me."

My eyebrows went up. "Only you?"

"You do know that we're getting married one of these days, don't you?" He smirked.

"No, but thanks for the heads-up," I replied, laughing. It was the first I'd heard of it. But I dismissed it as a joke. I said good night and went back to the room, closing the door behind me. As I balled up under the sheets, I began to think of what Luca said. He'd never brought it up, and aside from us confessing our love, we hadn't really talked much about it. Wasn't there supposed to be a discussion or something first? I didn't know my father, so I never saw a married couple up close aside from Seraph and Gabriel. But they were different. They were like gravity: they finished each other's sentences; they could speak without words. The more I thought about them, the sadder I got. I missed them so much.

I walked through the waterfall and into the little cave and gasped as I looked around. Little lights lit up the entire area making the onyx walls cast rainbows across the room. Flowers hung in-between the lights as their petals floated gently to the ground. There was a furry rug in the middle covered with lots of pillows with candles sitting in the center. A picnic basket sat in the corner beside a bouquet of wildflowers. I looked at Luca who just stared at me smiling.

"You did all of this?" I kept looking at everything; it was so beautiful. He nodded as he helped me sit on the pillow.

"For me?" I was still in shock.

He laughed. "Who else would it be for?"

"Well, I don't know, I...wow." I didn't even know what to say.

"Shhh, sit sit." I sat on my pillow crossing my legs as he grabbed the picnic basket, placing it between us. He opened it up and revealed containers of food—pasta, salad, and garlic bread. My stomach growled as I watched the steam roll off the food. Then a thought struck me.

"When did you do all of this?" He pulled out plates and set one in front of us.

"It's a secret."

My mind ran over the events of the day. There was no way he could have done this by himself. I was practically with him all day. I kept staring at everything as he portioned out the food onto our plates. We said a prayer, then ate. I sighed with delight with every bite I took.

"Did you make this?" He nodded with his mouth full "This needs to be the next cooking lesson." He smiled, swallowing his food before sitting his plate back on the rug.

"Ora?"

"Yes?" He took a deep breath and let it out slowly. I sat my food down, giving him my full attention. He opened his mouth and quickly closed it, shaking his hand. "What's wrong?"

"I'm trying to figure out how to say this." He scratched his head.

"Just say it," I whispered.

He held my eyes for a second before speaking. "Ora, I love you."

I laughed. "That's what you were scared to say? I already know that. You told me, remember?"

"Well, that's not entirely it." I looked at him, waiting for him to finish. "I first started back in Verdea. I realized it after I saw that guy trying to talk to you." Now that was new information. "But I haven't always treated you the way you deserve. Back in Cauldron, when I said those things... Ora, you have no idea how much it hurt to say those things to you, but I needed you to stay away. I didn't want anything to happen to you. But I see now that I mishandled the situation. Yet even after that, you came to help me. Your persistence is one of the things I love about you." He glanced at me.

"Luca, I forgave you for that." I knew he only did it to protect me, and I'd long ago forgiven him. I didn't know he was still beating himself up about it.

"I know. I promise I will never do anything to hurt you like that ever again. You deserve the world. You're kindhearted, loving, compassionate, forgiving." He was talking fast now as if he was in a hurry to get it out.

"I don't think I can do life without you, and honestly, I don't want to," he confessed.

I gave him a heartwarming smile. "Neither do I."

He smiled at the ground as he grabbed my hand. "I know I'm not perfect, but I want to be for you. I got you something," he added, reaching behind his back for a little woven sack. I examined it as he handed it to me and looked inside. I pulled out a tiny box and opened it. Inside was a ring etched in gold. A large red stone sat in the middle surrounded by smaller orange ones. It was beautiful. I looked up at him.

"This is so nice," I said, making him laugh. He moved the plates out of the way and kneeled in front of me.

"Alora, I love you with every part of my being. You've shown me love, forgiveness, and even God, someone I thought left me long ago. He brought me to you so that you could bring me to him. And for that I thank you. You are more than I could ever want and, frankly, more than I deserve. But I promise to always make you as happy as you make me. Alora, will you marry me?" He held the ring up, smiling.

"Marry you? You want me to marry you?" My eyes were wide as I stared at him.

"Yes."

"But, Luca, I don't know how to be a wife."

"And I don't know how to be a husband. But we will learn together," he told me simply. And I knew he was right. Some things were learned through experience. I bit my lip.

"*Ndio.*" His smile widened as he put the ring on my left hand. I hugged him tightly, smiling myself. I knew that if God got us through before, he would get us through this.

ABOUT THE AUTHOR

A. R. Williams is a hopeless romantic who loves writing. So hopeless in fact that she created an entire fantasy world for your enjoyment in her debut novel, *Argo*.

A. R. is a college student who, after many years and several major changes, decided to follow her gut and study professional writing following her degree in studio/fine art.

She is also inspired by the romantic hero of her life, her husband, Zay-Qwan. Together they are raising the world's cutest baby girl, Alorah, in their Virginia home.

She is a devoted Christian in the Apostolic faith who believes that life is always better when you have Jesus leading you—a message she hopes to share with the world.